In Praise of Masturbation

In Praise of Masturbation

Philippe Brenot

Translated from the French
by Paul Buck & Catherine Petit

MARION BOYARS
LONDON • NEW YORK

First published in Great Britain and the United States in 2005 by
MARION BOYARS PUBLISHERS LTD
24 Lacy Road, London SW15 1NL

www.marionboyars.co.uk

Distributed in Australia and New Zealand by Peribo Pty Ltd
58 Beaumont Road, Kuring-gai, NSW 2080

10 9 8 7 6 5 4 3 2 1

A CIP catalogue record for this book is available from the British Library.
A CIP catalog record for this book is available from the Library of Congress.

ISBN 0-7145-3109-X

The publishers would like to thank the Arts Council of England for assistance with the translation of this book.

This book is supported by the French Ministry for Foreign Affairs, as part of the Burgess programme headed by the Institute Français du Royaume-Uni for the French Embassy in London.

Set in Sabon 11/14
Printed and bound by in the UK by Bookmarque, London.

Contents

Prelude

I confess here, openly, and as an act of atonement: 'Yes, I've masturbated...and several times too!'

This confession of a contemptible crime, this repeat offence, would have cost me my life under the Spanish Inquisition, would have merited prison in the 18th century, a flogging and corporal punishment in the 19th, and contempt and severe disapproval not so long ago. Today it leaves some people indifferent, while it offends those who still don't know what to think about it.

Ben Johnson confessed to doping himself, de Quincey admitted to taking opium and Gautier to smoking hashish. I confess to masturbation, a solitary crime if ever there was one, whose roots emerge from the divine precepts of the Bible; a crime that was reborn from its ashes in the 'Dark Ages' of the 18th century, not Rousseau's century but Tissot's, a fellow citizen from Geneva, who clumsily preached war on sex.

In 1758, with the publication of his treatise *On Onanism or The Ills Produced by Masturbation*, Tissot inaugurated two hundred years of obscurantism by proclaiming sexual repression, repression of dawning impulses and sexual guilt in what is the most 'imaginative', the most natural, the most necessary sexual act: masturbation. Over time, his discourse has become part of our morality. It still permeates language and popular thought today. It is still alive at the very centre of our uncertainties, it feeds the guilt of men, women and couples who believe secretly, in their innermost hearts, that what is good is bad.

Although it is the most frequent act of our sexuality, masturbation remains the most intimate taboo of western sexual morality. Morals have changed. Sex is shown on television. One can talk about rape, incest or transexuality, for it doesn't relate to most of us directly. I've never raped, I'll never be incestuous, I'm not about to change my sex, while...

This formidable crusade, led by an army of naïve persecutors, was in reality motivated, justified and even legitimatized by a very deep fear of the end of the world, and the total destruction of humanity, when faced by that distressing revelation: sperm is alive, it contains human beings, beware of genocide!

But if a vengeful sadism threw this criminal anathema at the whole world, nobody has yet dared to say that the prohibition has been lifted; that is, not until today with *In Praise of Masturbation*.

'Just for Sex'

It is good that the words which are least used, least written, and best kept silent are the best known and more generally acknowledged.

MONTAIGNE, *Essays*, III, 5.

As one can say something is done 'just for fun', I think one can use the phrase 'just for sex' in the same manner. Almost by chance, a crime was committed in the 18th century, in the Vaud district of Switzerland. This 'sex crime' happened in the melting pot of Europe on the banks of Lake Geneva where both Rousseau, a citizen of Geneva and Voltaire, from the hills of Ferney, excelled.

This idea of doing something 'just for sex' first came about in 1758 with the publication in Lausanne of a very serious book, written in Latin by Samuel Tissot, *Testamen de Morbis ex Manustupratione* ('A physical dissertation on the ills produced by masturbation'), which was published almost privately following on from one of his most famous texts, his *Dissertation on Bilious Fevers*.

As with many others at the time, that publication could have been nothing more than anecdotal. But it did however wake up the old demons of the Inquisition and witch hunts, and it influenced attitudes and sexual morality, lasting right up until the beginning of the 20th century. That symbolic book, which would continue to be re-published, provoked the biggest outbreak of sexual repression known to Europe, and one which still endures today.

Samuel Auguste David André Tissot, who always wrote his name preceded by the two initials S.A. (Samuel André), was born in Grancy in the Vaud district on March 20th 1728, to a very religious family. His uncle, who cared for him during his childhood, was a pastor. He succeeded brilliantly at school in Geneva, then studied medicine at Montpellier, the oldest and most reputable faculty of the day. A doctor by the year 1749, Tissot returned to settle in Lausanne, where he rapidly gained a reputation throughout Europe for his therapeutic skills, notably in his treatment of smallpox – which he cured with remedies termed 'laxatives' at a time when sweating alone was recommended – a counter-therapy which made him very famous. At the same time, Tissot published numerous books which caused a considerable stir because, for the first time, a doctor was writing for the people and was expressing his knowledge through popular language. His *Advice to the People with Regard to their Health*, published in 1761 and translated into ten languages, brought him the praise of his fellow doctors. Lausanne made him a burgher and a member of the Council. Berne and Geneva awarded him numerous honours. The Royal Society in London made him one of its members. In 1786, the King of Poland offered him the title of 'First Doctor', a title he also received the following year from the King of England.

Tissot refused these honours and stayed in Lausanne where people came from all over Europe to consult him. His medico-literary work was sufficiently original to gain the interest of a very large public. Alongside specialized books on fevers, migraine or epilepsy, and following his *Advice to the People with Regard to their Health*, he published first a very modern reflection on the anguish of literary people, *On Diseases Incident to Literary and Sedentary Persons*, in 1769, followed, the next year, by his *Essay on the Illnesses of the People of Society*, a kind of manual of popular medicine for the upper classes.

In the light of this list of achievements, Tissot appeared to be an an exceptional man: original, inventive, and a tireless worker endowed with an unquestionable charisma. He had obviously no need of sex to exist, nor to give him a reputation. He was already at that time famous for his medical reputation. Today he is only famous for what he said on masturbation.

If Tissot appears today to have been the great demiurge of this 'just for sex', the all-powerful creator of the myth of masturbation, the actual situation is somewhat different. In reality, Tissot was only the amplifying echo of a traumatic shock – the discovery of spermatozoa by pre-scientific Europe and the revelation of the mysteries of life – who reacted to it defensively by forbidding masturbation. The scapegoat always has the virtue of reinforcing the unity of a society in crisis. And here the case was of a sexual crime, which transgressed the supreme taboo, that of the preservation of life. For a persecution to be legitimate, the victim must be shown to be guilty of the crime of which he stands accused. So the persecution will be complete when it has survived from one generation to another, at the vengeful hands of those that René Girard cynically called the 'naïve persecutors', 'those who don't know what they're doing.'

As in all criminal history, the chronology of facts was enlightening and confirmed the hypothesis of a medico-religious conspiracy aimed at preserving the fertility of the species. A century earlier, before the crime took place, masturbation was no more condemned by the Church than it was by society, which only condemned the excesses of debauchery. Proof, if proof be needed, of this 'indifference' with regard to masturbation can be found in the famous *Mysteries of Conjugal Love Reveal'd* by Nicolas Venette. This is the very first 'sex manual', published in 1675, and it doesn't once mention the term 'masturbation'.

The outstanding event, the event that unleashed this idea of 'just for sex', was in reality the discovery of spermatozoa by Leeuwenhoek in 1677, a discovery that overwhelmed the scientists and philosophers of the time, for they had to rethink sexual morality taking into account this new and surprising perspective. The discovery was followed a few years later by the publication in London, in 1710, of an anonymous pamphlet, attributed by Tissot to a certain Doctor Bekkers, and called *Onania or the Heinous Sin of Self-pollution and All its Frightful Consequences in Both Sexes Considered with Moral and Physical Counsels Addressed to those already Prejudiced by that Abominable Habit*. This work also enjoyed considerable success, Voltaire counting up to twenty-four editions only a few years after its initial publication. In no time the European medical world adopted an unanimous position: all the great doctors – Boerhaave, Hoffmann, Blancard, Lewis, Zimmermann – expressed concordant opinions and condemned masturbation. Tissot then published his *Testamen* in 1758. It was translated into French two years later and appeared alongside another book, from the same publisher in Lausanne, *Onanism or the Moral and Philosophical Discourse on Artificial Lust and All its Relative Crimes*. It was written by a pastor, Dutoit-Membrini, an influentual preacher who would become the 'guru' of an extreme sect, and who clearly complemented Tissot's discourse. This infernal duo had obviously premeditated the crime: 'I write on diseases which are the result of masturbation and not on the crime of masturbation,' said Tissot. 'I will try to contemplate the moral side and show all its horror,' Membrini added. The crusade against sex had begun.

Two centuries earlier, in 1576, at his château, not far from where his mayoral seat in Bordeaux would be, Michel Eyquem de Montaigne wrote the final words of his *Apology for Raymond Sebond*, the twelfth chapter of the second book of his *Essays*, a long, free criticism of the facts and everyday banalities of good sense. Montaigne permitted himself to contradict the classical philosophers and the ideas of his time under the guise of a defense of a famous contemporary Spanish theologian. In the very last pages of the chapter he wrote about the relativity of moral values, vice and virtue, and noted, for the first time in the French language, the word 'masturbation': 'For Diogenes, practising masturbation in public was expressing the wish, before by-standers, that he could satiate thus his belly by rubbing it.' (II, 12).

The history of the word is a curious one, a scholarly derivative from the Latin that appeared from the pen of Montaigne in a period when language was re-inventing itself according to the mood of the times and beneath the weight of new ideas. Raised with Latin as a living language, it seemed quite probable that Montaigne thus became the creator of the word and, consequently, in some way, the inventor of the concept in French. One does not speak of masturbation with impunity.

Can we speak of Montaigne the free-thinker? Or rather about a thinker free of all dogmatism, who made light of morality and preferred a personal ethic derived from personal experience, making him one of the first to allow himself to oppose the opinions of the moralists. He added: 'To those who asked him (Diogenes) why he didn't seek a more suitable place to eat (masturbate) than the middle of the street, he answered, because I am hungry in the middle of the street.' Montaigne defended individual freedom, though with this one restriction: 'Let them apply no other bridle to their pleasures than the moderation and preservation of the freedom of others.' (*op. cit.*)

It was symbolically significant that this word was born from the pen of Montaigne when we know of the moral commitment of the author of the *Essays* to true confession in the face of the silence of others: 'Besides, I commanded myself to dare to say everything that I dare to do, and I do not appreciate thoughts considered unpublishable... For it is good that the words which are least used, least written and best kept silent, are the best known and more generally acknowledged.' (III, 5) This statement was a first confession.

The word was to be successfully received in two forms which would coexist for more than a century: '*manustupration*' (from the Latin '*manus*', the hand, and '*stupratio*', the act of defilement) and '*masturbation*' (from the Latin '*masturbatio*', though perhaps from the Greek '*mastropeuein*', to prostitute), with, nevertheless, rare and even confidential useage, for masturbation was not yet the object of any condemnation and there was no reason to talk about it, not, as some 19th century doctors naïvely believed, because it didn't exist at the time(!), but rather because of the natural place it held in maturing and in sexual blossoming.

A trail of popular or metaphorical terms can be found in 17th century literature. There is the famous phrase, 'I sharpen my knife for tonight,' from a tale by La Fontaine, and also the well-known phrase by Tallemant des Réaux: 'I think, madam,' he said, 'you are congratulating yourself'. Or another, the lines from Alexis Piron's *Ode to Priapus*: '...good Guillot saw it stiffen/ And gripped so strong by concupiscence/ That in a corner manualized.' But the word was still not to be found in the pages of the dictionary: it is conspicuous by its absence in the first edition of the *Dictionnaire de l'Académie* in 1694. Thanks to the painstakingly laborious work of the French Academy, it didn't make its grand appearance until the Sixth Edition – in 1835! Without assuming them all assiduous masturbators, it was very unlikely that anyone was unaware of the word. But we were still in the 17th century, pre-Leeuwenhoek, and nobody had anything to say against masturbation.

Christian morality condemned the sin of the flesh and its excess; lust. So the faculty of medicine followed in the steps of the clergy. Thereafter doctors and theologians voiced the same opinion, first they condemned 'lust', then they castigated 'the solitary vice'. Numerous authors have attempted to explain the reason behind that repressive outburst. Some have forwarded a sociological argument, suggesting that the evolution of human society required greater control of natural instincts. Others have explained it as a collective repression seeking to reinforce morals that were too loose, or as a guilt complex that would thus be rectified. Personally I believe that the masturbator was a scapegoat who in fact only existed to conceal the deep-seated reasons for that repressive tendency, as one hides a great fear or a strong guilt complex.

In 1675, only two years before Leeuwenhoek, Nicolas Venette mentioned masturbatory behaviour a few times in his *Mysteries of Conjugal Love Reveal'd*, but without ever calling it by name, or condemning the practise. 'She is a brunette whose sparkling eyes are the marks of a hidden flame. Her mouth is pretty and well-drawn, though slightly large and dry, her nose a bit flat and snub. Her chest is big and firm, her voice strong and her hips wide. Her hair is black, long and a little coarse and since the age of eleven or twelve she has noticed hair sprouting from her natural parts, and sensual emotions stirred there. One would rather drain the sea or pick the stars with one's hands than break the bad leanings of this young girl. Her nature, her beauty, her health and her youth are great obstacles to her chastity, and all of that was useful to teach her how to love tenderly.' No condemnation was attached to this observation. One even got the feeling that Venette considered sexual impulses the guarantee of a freer love life. What could one do, he asked, against the power of desire? One would rather drain the sea! The repressive wave hadn't yet been born.

Only a few years later, the same story would sound completely different. 'This disease attacks young or libidinous people. They don't have a fever and, although they eat well, they lose weight and waste away... Pleasure always harms the weak and its frequent practise weakens the strongest.' Each page abounded in apoplexies, lethargies, epilepsies, tremblings, debilities, nervous irritations and emaciations which were only the natural consequences of the most odious crime, the crime against nature: masturbation. This was in 1758, post-Leeuwenhoek, in the first lines of Tissot's discourse.

As the pages flowed, pollution, masturbation and debauchery blended in a ballet of guilt which unleashed the methodical disorder of each part of the body, of the least of its organs; which drained the strengths and dried up fluids, which exhausted the body and soul.

The first scene he paints is a very famous one today for it has been used again and again, like an echo, for nearly two centuries. It has the merit – and sole merit – of being very frightening: 'I was myself scared,' Tissot confessed, 'the first time I saw the unfortunate man. Then I felt the necessity to show young people all the horrors of the abyss into which they threw themselves voluntarily.'

L.D. was a clockmaker. He had enjoyed good health until he was seventeen years old. It was at that time that he surrendered to masturbation, a vice he would repeat every day, as much as three times a day, and the ejaculation was always accompanied by a very expressive apocalypse, Tissot specified, a slight loss of consciousness and a convulsive movement of the extensor muscles of the head 'which drew it firmly backwards while the neck bulged extraordinarily'.

The picture was impressive, the tone alarmist. The warning was clear, the prognosis vital. 'Before a year had slipped by,' he continued, 'he began to experience great weakness after each act. This warning was not enough to drag him out of the mire. His soul, already surrendered to this filth, was no longer capable of any other ideas, and the repetitions of his crime became daily more frequent, until he was in a state that made him fear death. Too late for wisdom, the disorder had already made so much progress that he couldn't be cured, and the genital organs had become so irritable and weak that the unfortunate man didn't need to perform another act for his semen to issue. The slightest irritation caused an imperfect erection, immediately followed by the evacuation of that liquor which increased each day his weakness. That spasm, which he only used to experience when he was perpetuating the act, had now become regular and attacked him without any apparent cause, and in such a violent manner that during an entire attack, which could sometimes last fifteen hours, he felt pains so violent that he was not shouting, but screaming. It was impossible for him then either to eat or drink anything.

His voice had become hoarse…and he totally lost his strength. Forced to renounce his professional activity, overwhelmed with misery and incapable of anything, he languished almost helplessly for a few months, all the more to be pitied; for some remnants of memory – which soon also disappeared – served to constantly remind him of the cause of his misfortune, and to increase the horror of his remorse.'

'Having learned of his state, I went to see him,' Tissot continued. 'I found less a living being than a corpse lying on the straw; thin, pale, dirty, giving off a foul stench, almost incapable of moving. From his nose flowed a pale, watery blood. Spit constantly issued from his mouth. Attacked by diarrhoea, he produced excrement in his bed without even realizing it. The flow of his semen was continual. His rheumy, bleary, dulled eyes no longer had the power to move. His pulse was extremely weak and fast, his breathing very uncomfortable, the emaciation excessive, except for the feet that had become swollen with fluid. The disorder of the spirit was no less, he was without ideas, without memories, incapable of stringing two sentences together, without reflection without anxiety for his fate, without any other feeling other than that of his pain. Well beneath the state of an animal, a vision whose horror one cannot conceive, one has trouble acknowledging that he used to belong to the human race. He died a few weeks later, in June 1757, his entire body swollen with fluid.'

Like many observations, that one had all the attributes of a parable. It began with a moving testimony: 'I was myself scared,' which alone authenticated the story, and gave it credibility and a sense of the truth, as if to say: 'What I am going to tell you is true!'

The grandiloquent description and the dramatization of the story contributed to create a suggestive atmosphere which allowed readers to assent to the conclusions of the 'good doctor Tissot' when even he himself – and everybody knew of his great proficiency – couldn't do anything against such a plague. He could then deliver the *coup de grâce*: 'Not all of those who commit themselves to that odious and criminal habit are so cruelly punished, but there are none who aren't affected to some degree.'

There is no reason to doubt Tissot's sincerity, but there is also no reason to assent to his conclusions. The picture here was clearly that of an acute case, with serious developments, most probably a generalized toxic infection whose end proved fatal in the absence of a specific treatment, but which had no link with the possible practice of masturbation.

Which sensible man or woman would now dare to touch their sexual organs after such a vivid description! How many inhibitions and anxieties, how much guilt had been knowingly roused by generations of standardizing and moralizing doctors.

'I will show the extent of this crime,' Membrini added in his *Onanism*, 'I will dig into its sources, I will make you see how it is superior in viciousness to the simple and natural act of fornication, itself already so criminal... It is an infernal epidemic that spreads its infection from one to the other. How could we not set some counter-poison against this cup of seduction, presented by so many ambassadors of the enemy, and that our youth receives and gives in turn.' And he continued, as if it was necessary: 'Youth, already unfortunately guilty, after having seen in the previous book (Tissot's) the frightening infirmities of a body you cherish, contemplate here again the condemnation which awaits you if you don't take the swiftest measures to draw you back from that abyss.'

Obviously those two books had been written at the same time, with the complementary purpose of physical and moral repression of sexual impulses, in a rivalry of ideas which sometimes bordered on delirium. Let us not forget that Tissot received encouragement and congratulations from all over, that Rousseau claimed to be his friend, and Voltaire, his close neighbour, who spent several winters in Lausanne, thanked him: 'This book is a favour done for humanity. My letter would be longer if I surrendered myself to the feelings of high esteem that I hold you in... Your patient, Voltaire.'

Rousseau forgot his solitary practice for the time being and expressed guilt-ridden regrets: 'Very annoyed not to have known sooner the treatise *On Masturbation*... You tell me that this book has been prohibited in Paris. That would comfort me – for mine (*Émile*) has been burnt there – if stupidity and sanctimoniousness, in justifying what they blame, didn't show the shame and misery of our species... I know that we are made for each other, you and me, for understanding and loving each other. All those who think like us are friends and brothers... I am at your feet, Monsieur.' (July 1762)

Rousseau, who would be supportive of him at all times, never tired of praising the 'doctor of the soul', as he used to call him, whom he wanted to have as his final confident: 'How much I would like, in my last days sickness, to have Tissot at my side, so that when there is nothing more to do for the body, he may still be the doctor of the soul' (1st April 1765).

In the same year, 1765, a very long article was published in the *Encyclopedia* entitled 'Manstupration' or 'Manustupration' that ran to six columns on four pages. To the theory of bodily fluids and their evacuation was now added the moral weight which attached itself to masturbation. 'The only way, according to the views of nature, to empty the superfluous semen, is what nature has established in the intercourse and union with women...and which it has sanctioned, in order to encourage its practice, with the most delicious delights... Despite these wise precautions of nature, one has seen...an infamous habit, born of indolence and idleness, spread and prevail... Those forced pleasures...are the cause of an infinite number of serious diseases, which are often fatal.' The usual fables from a monomaniac discourse follow, always with a tragic outcome; a few clinical cases from Tissot, including the one about the clockmaker; a debate on the opinion held by Hippocrates; and finally some therapeutic advice ranging from quinine to a change of scenery and, of course, abstinence. Mentalities had changed, repression had begun.

'Must we seek out the cause of masturbation in the vices of education, in the seduction of dangerous examples and in strong temperament or in the effect of passions?', Chambon de Montaux wondered in his treatise *On Girls' Diseases* in 1785, 'For the relationships formed through vice have almost always a seductive appearance.' In a few years the discourse had changed, the doctor had become a moralist and a inquisitor, the relationship was legitimate and the crime had been committed.

The Gift of Sperm

What a marvellous sight when he discovered those living animals!

LIGNAC, *Man and Woman*, 1772.

A fundamental historic mistake, this phrase 'just for sex' seemed to have been built around a misunderstanding: the confusion between onanism and masturbation through an erroneous interpretation of seminal loss.

The story of Onan is widely known, but few people have actually paid attention to its content. In Genesis (XXXVIII) Onan was the second son of Judah, one of the founders of the tribe of Israel. As a patriarch who ruled his family, Judah chose wives for his sons, just as he would for himself:

'Judah took a wife for Er his first-born, and her name was Tamar. But Er, Judah's first-born, was wicked in the sight of the Lord; and the Lord slew him. Then Judah said to Onan, "Go to your brother's wife, and perform the duty of a brother-in-law to her, and raise up offspring for your brother." But Onan knew that the offspring would not be his; so when he went to his brother's wife he spilled the semen on the ground, lest he should give offspring to his brother. And what he did was displeasing in the sight of the Lord, and he slew him also.'

More than one meaning can be made of that biblical text. First, an ironic one: this is a very old-fashioned type of family story which is intended to make us feel guilty, but everyone realises this no longer relates to us. Second, a pseudo-analytic one: one can read the revolt of the sons against the law of the Father, who bonds with God in order to exercise his punishment. Had they committed such a great offence to deserve death as punishment? Their offence was to have displeased, to have revolted against God and the Father who pronounced an iniquitous law, who married that son against his will and dispossessed him of his child. One could pay tribute to Onan who, faced by that double constraint, had invented contraception, the first mention in history of *coitus interruptus*.

The classic reading of that chapter of Genesis sends us back to the old custom of levirate (from the Latin '*levir*', brother-in-law) – which was imposed on a childless young widow, and forced her to marry her brother-in-law – and to the condemnation of Onan for having wasted his semen. Even if we didn't know Er's offence, Onan's was very clear: he nipped in the bud his future children. The Hebrew term which is here translated by 'offspring' means both 'semen' and 'posterity'. It is still the position today of many Jewish and Christian fundamentalists who condemn all methods of contraception on the basis that it is a killing, a murder of descendants, for onanism is, under that name, nothing other than *coitus interruptus*.

The confusion between onanism and masturbation only appeared, it seems, with the publication of *Onania*, the book written by Bekkers, who used that term to anchor his moralistic discourse to the Bible, and to strike at the spirits. Clearly he is not talking about onanism in the literal sense, but of self-pollution, which means masturbation. Like its comrade 'masturbation', the term 'onanism' was not part of the dictionaries of the 18th century. It made a late entrance in the dictionary of the Academy in 1835 with the meaning of 'masturbation', each word echoing the other.

If onanism was in fact very different from the manual practise, confusion arose because of the proximity of the two meanings, both converging on the same result: the loss of semen. Like the use of contraception today, every method of diversion of sperm outside natural ways was violently condemned by Christian morality. Fertilizing intercourse was the only lawful kind in the eyes of the Church. The masturbator/onanist was thus reprehensible and could be condemned to death, for the same reason as Onan: he let life escape.

We can recall nevertheless that this condemnation was an old one, part of the confusion of the humoral theory which blended blood, lymph and sperm into one single internal liquid, synonymous with life. 'Man's semen,' Hippocrates said, 'comes from all his body fluids, it is the most important part of it.' As with blood, sperm was then considered as an entire part of the human body, like flesh, to such an extent that that question divided the first Christians, some accepting fellation as a kind of fraternal communion – this is my body – while others condemned it as cannibalism. In his *Of Semen*, one of the fathers of medicine, Galenus, pursued the same idea: 'That fluid is only the most subtle part of all the others, its veins and nerves carry it from the whole body to the testicles. In losing his semen, the man loses his vital spirit too. It is thus not surprising that too frequent coitus weakens, since it deprives the body of what is purest in it.' That old belief of the equivalence between humours and their internal mixing will be in force for two thousand years. Sexual excess was understood then as a cause for loss of energy.

The 17th century was a century of invention, the invention of language, but also of techniques. As soon as Jansen, the Dutch scientist, invented the microscope in 1604, observations abounded, but nothing very notable happened for seventy years – everything observed was inert, static, lifeless – until Leeuwenhoek discovered, in 1677, what he first called 'animalcules' and which are today our spermatozoa, pride of the male species if one takes into account the success of some recent movies featuring this masculine prototype.

Leeuwenhoek's great amazement on the one hand was measured against the infinitesimally small things which he discovered on the other. They resembled bisexual tadpoles, he said, but above all that 'sometimes more than a thousand move in a space as small as a grain of sand.' This unsuspected life in the heart of the genital liquid and the importance of that multitude seemed to have deeply impressed the naturalists who studied the spermatic animal. It's necessary to note that spermatozoa was then considered as a complete little being waiting to grow. What could be done, faced with that discovery; that crowd, that multitude doomed to 'God knows what' – life, suicide or extermination?

In 1772, in his *Treatise on Man and Woman*, Lignac gave evidence of the perplexity felt by the naturalist facing these new questions posed by nature: 'Hartsoeker decided to examine the seminal liquor under the microscope. What a marvellous sight when he discovered those living animals! One drop was an ocean in which an innumerable multitude of small fish swam in a thousand different directions... One could scarcely prevent oneself from thinking that these animals discovered in the male fluid were those which one day must reproduce him. And following that discovery, fertilization is entirely up to men.'

The first obvious fact that came to the minds of these pioneers was that the animal was pre-formed in the sperm, then developed in the uterus. Another vanity: man alone would thus ensure the descent of humanity! That thesis, formulated by Leeuwenhoek and the first spermaticians, which supported in a sense the masculine primacy, was opposed to the thesis of a great anatomist, another Dutchman called Régnier de Graaf, who had just discovered the ovaries, and maintained that the embryo was entirely contained in them. 'The male semen is nothing else than the vehicle of a volatile and animal spirit which impresses on the female ovum a vital contact.' Each was capable of seeing only his own theory; the fertilizing role played by the spermatozoa would not be proven until the end of the 19th century.

Lignac had not finished marvelling: 'Leeuwenhoek, in his wonderful observations, found that those animalcules are so tiny and so numerous that 3,000,000,000 are not equal to a grain of sand. Moreover, this famous physician saw the male and the female! Those animals have a tail and look quite similar to frogs.' Those ethnologists from another planet were travellers of the imaginary. They discovered, built and invented according to the whims of their imagination. Some thought they had seen the figure of a man in the shape of a worm, others claimed to be able to distinguish between males and females. All of them observed the multitude and extreme agitation which was the sign of life. Why then did we find movement only in the seminal liquid? The scientists had looked closely at other liquors from the human body, but all seemed desperately lifeless. At best, a few big inert corpuscles glided on 'still deserted seas where no sign of life is observed'.

These travellers of that infinitesimal world remained puzzled for nearly two centuries. But they never stopped wondering and the infinite number of their questions threw up more uncertainties than assurances of the truth. Anxiety and revulsion dominated the contradictory feelings of those who tried to understand what was still incomprehensible. First, it was the number, the multitude which amazed, confused, then disturbed: 'What ought to shock our sense of the rational more is the strange disproportion between the number of these little beings contained in one seminal drop, and the number of beings who are born.'

'Immense richness!' Maupertuis exclaimed, 'boundless

fecundity of Nature, aren't you here an over-abundance?' Imagination knows no limit when one has to explain the unexplainable. Isn't this miniature world a replica of the other, the human one? And since when did it have the ability to live without us knowing? Since creation? Are those spermatic animals immortal? Is their number constant, equal even to that of all humanity? Further still, if each of us contains an infinity of generations, shouldn't we think, continued Lignac, that 'Adam would have contained all the men that appeared on the earth and all of those still to inhabit it?... The first man would thus have contained the seeds of all the men to be born in the future.' Madness was at its peak, reason reached its end: 'There isn't even a young man or a young woman about whom one couldn't say the same.' This is the consummation of the crime of Onan; catastrophy is imminent. Because of one single guilty ejaculation, the murder of humanity is now possible. Alarmist discourses spread like wildfire in an apocalyptic atmosphere. The vision of 'the total annihilation of organized beings' appeared beneath the eye of the microscope.

In the light of that hypothesis we can really re-read many onanist texts. The murder of humanity and the threat of the end of the world suddenly appeared in filigree in the discourses of all moralizers: 'To lose one's seeds, to displace them,' said Membrini, 'is to suppress their destination, to make them totally useless, to violate the law of Nature, the law of God...it is no less than to annihilate the system of creation.'

The agony of death and its origin in the revelation of a spermatic life clearly appeared with the founders of the crusade against masturbation. It was Membrini who blamed onanism, here called the '*enormous*': 'Here it is, the *enormous*, guilty of both suicide and infanticide. But who could calculate the number of murders? How many beings disposed of? To understand these questions, there is one thing to know: that one man would be capable, by himself, of producing such a number of beings that our planet would have difficulty containing them.' 'Is it not adequate in proving this activity a crime,' responded Tissot, 'to demonstrate that it is a suicidal act?' In that case, the Apocalypse was not far and eternal damnation lay in wait for all men who enjoyed the pleasures of life, all sensualists, all men and women beaming with sexual fulfilment but, above all, guilty of that abominable act. It would seem that the sad, the shy, the inhibited, the repressed were to be spared; all those who, suffused with a halo, have been blessed with the virtue of chastity.

Offensive as it might be to moralizers, the sperm bank has been invented to mitigate nature's deficiencies. So arm yourself with a sterilized flask and an offer of paternity: onanism, that sad loss of semen, is forbidden by the Church, but not masturbation, which cultivates the furtherance of the species!

The Doctors of Love

Are we going to jeopardize progress, are we going to let the machines rust because of ejaculations?

Doctors of love, doctors of death. Is that what we can call those persecutors who, for decades, have hunted down desire, smothered pleasure and killed love? As soon as the war on sex was declared, the reasons were forgotten and all arguments were valid, even the most absurd, the most sadistic, and the least thought out. One could really talk here about collective persecution in the same way as René Girard; the violence committed by murderous crowds 'like the massacre of the Jews during the Black Death.' Those words are not too strong, for that persecution of several generations killed that which the human soul was based upon, that which distinguished man from beast. For a time, it killed eroticism.

The witch hunt still possessed all the characteristics and stereotypes of collective persecution: the legitimacy which was lent by the medico-religious authority and the encouragement of public opinion. Europe had just come out of religious wars and its paranoia, for a while anaesthetized, needed only the most trivial of excuses to be reawakened. The 'hand of God', then, armed all the educators, instructors and teachers while the watchful eyes of the parents lacked vigilance. It armed the priest, the pastor and the cult leader with the ammunition they needed to make them respect the law of Modesty. It helped the doctor to follow the law of Nature.

We could talk about 'naïve' persecutors, in the face of the stupidity of their arguments and their questions. First it was the question of origin that perplexed them: how could such a practice, such a deep abomination, be born? Where and when? It seemed that they had never been in touch with their innermost being. 'It is difficult,' Doctor Fournier told us in 1893, 'to determine when this vice was born. It seems it was known in earliest Antiquity...but, comparing the vigour of the Ancients to ours, we have every reason to believe that onanism was less common at their time than it is in our Modern times.'

One has to be a very mediocre observer of nature to ask oneself such questions, considering masturbation is a behaviour common to both man and animals and is expressed in all human populations.

Fournier pursued his discriminatory thought: 'The inhabitants of the North are less prone to masturbation than those of the South, and that difference can be explained by the ardour of the climate, which in itself draws people to venereal excesses. Besides, it's principally in Africa and the southern countries of Asia that adults are familiar with the practice of onanism.' If that 'depraved' attitude seemed to him more frequent away from civilization, he also took up the widely prevalent idea of the time: that it was natural for primitives but unhealthy for civilization: 'The diseases produced by the excesses of onanism become more frequent as modern societies reach a higher level of civilization.'

Those who were intent upon repressing masturbation were unfazed by the contradictions or illogicalities inherent in their arguments. They blindly pursued their goal of eradicating evil wherever it was to be found. In the same way as the beginning of Christianity had been marked – in the manner of Paul or Augustine – by the rigorous principles of a few frustrated men who imposed morals of inhibition for centuries to come, the prescribers of that witch hunt didn't seem to have had any experience of masturbation themselves – or at least they were very careful not to admit it – and justified *a posteriori* their frustration with the condemnation of other people. It is indeed very rare for a man never to have masturbated. It is only observed in cases of deep inhibition or severe neuroses. This leads us to believe that Tissot, Membrini, Surbled, Fournier and others were sufficiently neurotic and inhibited to become deaf and blind to elementary experiences.

The story now began to take on a mythical aspect, as some clinical pseudo-cases were gradually repeated and embellished, as well as some exemplary stories which were skillfully narrated with the aim of making an impression on people's minds. It was this 'unfortunate story', told by Fabrice Hilden, 'of a young man whose hand had been severed and who, while on his way to recovery, wanted to satisfy his desire without the participation of his wife. This young man produced an emission of semen which was immediately followed by several violent accidents, from which he died four days later.' What does that incredible fable mean to show us except that a single hand is enough to perpetrate the crime!

One also has to be wary of the perversion in girls, Lignac added, for 'the size of the clitoris, which sometimes equals and even outdoes that of the penis, has led women to abuse it with others. That's the reason why the clitoris has been called "men's contempt".' Sperm is not at stake any longer, the myth of the phallic woman springs up again; a woman who has all man's prerogatives, initiative and pleasure, and represents for those very reasons a serious social threat, the risk of a revolution, the reversal of values in other words. It is the same here: the arguments are strong. False, but impressive. It was the fact of the clitoris being equal and even outdoing in size the male organ which filled these women with endless desire. It was that guilty clitoris which had to be cut, burnt or castrated in order for sexual impulses to return to normality. Lignac continued: 'The clitoris is usually rather small, it starts to appear in girls at puberty and grows as they become older and as they gain an erotic disposition. The smallest voluptuous titillation makes it swollen and, in the union of sexual organs, it stiffens like the part that distinguishes the male. For its extreme sensitivity, it was called in Latin "*gaude mihi*" ("give me pleasure"), and Venette calls it "the fire" or "Love's frenzy".'

Beware of those deformed clitorises and their subversive power. It was said that a woman who had one as thick as a goose-neck was publicly whipped for having abused it. Here lay the real threat: women who could do without men and so be their their equal. They were called 'tribades', indulgers in 'frottage', and also 'French polishers'! Fortunately we have books of virtues which teach us morality and condemn onanism. Doctors, employers and educators must be vigilant, for the vice creeps in even where it would not be expected. Along with technical progress, a thousand new reasons for torment appeared. 'The use of the sewing machine,' Doctor Pouillet recounted at the beginning of the 20th century, 'is not only a cause of masturbation, it's also a means. During a visit I made one day to a military dress factory, I witnessed the following scene. Among the unwavering noise of about thirty sewing machines, I suddenly heard one of those machines functioning at a higher speed than the others. I looked at the person operating it. She was an eighteen to twenty year old brunette. While she pushed through the trousers that she was making up automatically, her face was animated, her mouth slightly opened, her hands distended, and the backward and forward motion of her feet carried along the pedals at an ever-increasing speed. Soon I saw her eyes roll, her eyelids drop, her face grow pale and her head loll backwards, her hands and legs stop to relax. A small stifled cry followed by a long sigh was lost in the workshop noise. The young woman remained in rapture for a few seconds, took out her handkerchief and wiped her temples where beads of sweat had formed, cast a shy, shameful and still slightly wild look around at her co-workers and went back to work.' If it was not intended as a condemnation, this depiction of self-love would be a most beautiful one. The tone is rather free, real and lively. I think I'm not far from believing that the author of those lines took some pleasure in contemplating mechanical love.

Female self-sufficiency indicates an independence that is not to men's liking. It signifies the reign of ersatz, substitution, compensation. Instrumental coitus reduces the male sexual organ to the rank of subordinate and condemns it to resemble the very lowest dildo. Chambon de Montaux attested to this in his *History of Illnesses in Women and Girls*: 'Some women assured me they had felt, aged five, six and seven, unbearable itchings. One of them, in order to dispel them, embraced the column of her bed and rubbed herself on it until grazed and bleeding. It is not rare to see children tormented by an agitation which appears with the motion of walking, or those who fidget on their chairs. But the pain becomes sensual pleasure and the practice of masturbation remains.' With civilization the tools become more varied, as the imagination knows no limits. These are the 'foreign bodies' that doctors remove from their vaginal prisons, 'Sometimes parts of boxes,' Doctor Jaf told us in his curious *Physiology of Vice*, 'pins, knitting needles, pieces of straw, vegetables, candles, bits of wood, perfume bottles, crystal stoppers and corks…' But men are not to be left behind and, to imitate nature, 'depraved young men who have a rough idea of coitus introduce their penis into any old body,' he continued. 'Some have been seen using mattresses or pillows in which they had made a hole. Others have used natural cavities found in trees. Butchers' apprentices ejaculate into a calf liver, still warm and perforated for that use.'

If that was not enough, there is something even more unbearable and more subversive; the invisible part of the crime, the elusive quality of this unnatural act: the imagination. For what fundamentally differentiates masturbation from coitus is the substitution of a partner by fantasy, and what distinguishes its practice is the unverifiable and immoderate use of that fantasy. The most dangerous subversion takes place in the imagination. 'Moderate coitus is useful,' Tissot said, 'when nature demands it. When demanded by the imagination, it weakens all of the faculties of the soul.'

An obsession with these foul thoughts constantly occupies the mind of the demon, everywhere, at all times, 'In the middle of the most serious occupations, even acts of Religion, he is prey to desires and lustful ideas that never leave him alone.' Daring to think about the act of sex in church could even be tantamount to performing it! The persecutors' imaginations are just as bad as the crimes they denounce.

The sentence is cruel, but the judgement is certain: 'It will not be difficult to prove that you experienced only a *spurious pleasure*.' These are the words of an expert, Coffin Rosny, former pupil at the Hôtel-Dieu and author of a famous book, *Nature Outraged by the Deviations of Imagination*. 'The human being who is unhappy or depraved enough to surrender to this odious habit, and who is solely abandoned to his filthy meditations, experiences the same ills as a man of letters who fixes his mind on one single question. And this kind of excess rarely does no damage.'

Rosny took up the idea that Tissot denounced in his *On Diseases Incident to Literary and Sedentary Persons:*

the obsessive activity of the writer, comparable in a way to the onanist in what was later called 'intellectual masturbation'. This term was not yet fashionable but another was invented, 'mental onanism', to condemn the deviations of the imagination. 'What represents real mental onanism,' Doctor Buglé specified in his *Safety of the Sexual Organs* in 1909, 'is the agitation provoked by certain circumstances. Young girls speak about a young man whom they fancy. They make a wager between themselves as to who will blush first while thinking about the young man. The wager is taken, silence descends, each gazes into space, impressing on their minds the image of the young man. Arms folded, legs extended, motionless. After two, three, four or five minutes at the most, one of them blushes, feels herself moisten. She has carried off the prize for imaginative nervous activity.'

Sex is made reprehensible when the physical and moral balance of society is upset. In 1868, Louis Bergeret invented a phrase to describe this: he spoke of the 'frauds in the accomplishment of generative functions'. These genetic 'frauds' are harmful to society in two complementary ways: they are a cause for demoralization, and, above all, a cause for the fall in the birthrate. 'The ills generated by the vice I fight against have already reached the attention of others before they reached mine. Some pessimistic authors, some austere moralists have pretended that these genetic frauds 'lead our society to the abyss'. They willingly utter the cry of the poet witness of Rome's decline.' The threat is certain, it will be denounced a hundred times. 'Masturbation undermines social order, it loosens or even destroys married life, then moves on to attack the family – the essential basis of all society,' Doctor Lallemand declared in his *Treatise on Involuntary Seminal Loss* in 1838, immediately followed by this alarmist cry: 'Are we going to jeopardize progress, are we going to let the machines rust because of ejaculations?'

The end of the world is near if debauchery and vice are allowed to exist. 'This abominable practice has killed more beings than the bloodiest wars combined with the most depopulating epidemics.' It was again a Doctor, this time Doctor Debourge, who made this claim in 1860. Worse than that, Tissot went on, it is downright suicide: 'Allow me to pose a question here: those who kill themselves with a gunshot, who voluntarily drown themselves or cut their own throats, are they any more suicide victims than these men?'

Our vigilance must be on the alert at all times. It must hunt them down, spy on them, restrain them. 'A young prince was wasting away daily without anybody being able to discover the cause of his bad health,' confirmed Lignac. 'His surgeon suspected something, spied on him and caught him in the act. The habit was so strong that nothing could eradicate it. The disease worsened, he was losing his strength and was only saved because he was watched over day and night for more than eight months.' The signs that betray bad habits are well known: boredom, sadness, daydreaming, fatigue, agitation, insomnia, coughing, vomiting, itching, paleness, weight-loss...and above all, the now famous 'bags under the eyes' which have allowed the certain distinction of the guilty; anxious from sleepless nights. In a word, the symptoms prove everything and nothing, they are enough to confuse the people one wants to confuse, all the more because they are sensitive about it and one has the upper hand on them. Masturbation has thus formed a very convenient tool to cause a guilt complex and to take revenge for generations of adults frustrated as a result of sexually repressive morality.

How to be cured of sex?

Among the remedies for solitary love, the virtues of language have always formed an antidote to guilt complexes. It was called 'confession', made necessary by people who had been caught in the act. Facing the terrifying spectre brandished by the doctors of death, the guilty person confesses out of the desire to live. 'I had the misfortune, like so many young men, to take up a habit harmful to the body and soul,' a young man confessed to Tissot. 'When I was very young, I acquired a horrible habit that has ruined my health,' another confirmed. 'I can feel,' a third wrote, 'that this bad action has diminished my strength, and especially my memory.' The judgement resounds like thunder: 'I warned him to refrain from that vile debauchery and to remember the threat from the Eternal One who excludes the weak from the Kingdom of Heaven... How many have perished without ever daring to reveal the cause of their ills!'

As everything was fit to condemn, everything was fit to heal. The imagination was fertile enough to heal the sin of weakness. One of the first therapeutic weapons, which certainly would have discouraged and repressed more than one person, was the spectre of downfall which was conscientiously waved before the eyes of sexual delinquents. Potions, ointments, medications and hygenic rules followed, and then apparatus, preventive devices, protective methods, sheaths and safety barriers. Finally, the extreme measures, when nothing worked: surgery, extraction, removal.

The pretext of this treatment was almost certainly the indirect cause of the witch hunt since, according to Tissot, Bekkers was not a doctor but just a charlatan who sought to peddle his claptrap and to sell his potions. Anyway, the pretext of onanism allowed him to make a fortune from all of Europe. People came to London to be cured by the 'reinvigorating tincture' or the 'prolific powder' that one could obtain with *Onania* at the local bookseller, for the very reasonable price of twelve shillings!

Faced with the extent of this repressive wave, remedies bloomed, each trying to outdo the other. There were tranquillizers, sedatives, remedies to repress passion, antispasmodics (or so-called). Some recommended narcotics, hypnotics, and sleeping pills which, by deadening the body, deadened lust too. There was mandrake, that herb for hanged men, well-known for all sexual matters, and belladonna, beautiful Italian lady, henbrane, the 'apple of love'. There was also opium, camphor and nenuphar. Also, not forgetting agnus castus, that shrub, 'whose scent fought amorous thoughts and brushed aside lascivious daydreams,' and that was used to stuff the bed in order to preserve virtue. Leeches were applied on the genital area to calm down the sexual organ, allegedly blocked by sexual desire. Several counsels on hygiene were neatly added to this unusual pharmacopoeia: to take a cold bath at least three times a day with iron filings and a dash of cinnamon, and, above all, to avoid long stays in bed, too soft a bed, inactivity, idleness, overly tight trousers, suspicious friends and licentious writings. All remedies full of common sense when one knows the sin of weakness.

The 19th century being a technical century, the masturbatory surge created opportunities for numerous inventions and a flourishing industry in preventative devices. The most famous was the anti-onanism corset of Doctor Lafond – a tight-fitting bandage said to be 'infallible' – intended to prevent any touching. The ostensible purpose of such a device was to 'conceal the organs of reproduction under layers which, while allowing the excretion of urine, resisted onanism.' At the base of this equipment, a precious casket in the shape and size of the genitals boxed the sex in gold or silver to protect it from temptation. An English doctor, Doctor Milton, even recommended a securely locked chastity belt for the day and a penile ring furnished with erectile points for the night. These vigilant points were made to wake up the young man at the slightest erection. He was then under instruction to wash with cold water until the erection disappeared, and to replace the ring for a peaceful night. A terrible punishment when one knows that nocturnal erections are natural, daily and involuntary.

But there is only one true remedy, Doctor Tissot

reminded us. 'The most effective preventative, the only infallible one is to keep an eye on the young man, don't leave him alone day or night and make sure to sleep in his bedroom.' Doctor Demeaux looked for a technical solution to that daily problem and registered the patent of an extremely ingenious apparatus allowing the arrangement of special dormitories for adolescents in which the head and arms were separated from the rest of the body by a solid wood partition preventing all inclination to touch oneself. Unfortunately for the defenders of progress, his plans never made it off the drawing board.

In the end, the best results were obtained by electrotherapy and surgery. For if the impulse itself cannot easily be repressed, it is surely much easier to suppress the body part from which the impulse stems. Circumcision, castration, clitoridectomy, cauterization of the genital area with a red-hot iron or with electricity, or of the area of the internal shameful nerves – those which command genital sensitivity and erection – all were practised in total ignorance of the facts, even though it had been noticed that castration didn't abolish desire. 'This part (the clitoris) can be amputated,' Lignac said, calmly, 'at least its tip can, and it is even a religious act ordered by some people. In our countries, under some circumstances, a great number of girls would be made healthier if the living feeling of the clitoris could be dulled.'

The sadly famous observation of a Turkish doctor, Démétrius Zambaco, published in Paris in the serious scientific journal, *l'Encéphale*, in 1882, represented the paroxysm of this sadistic outburst. It is the almost unbearable account of the treatment of two young sisters aged eight and ten, who indulged in onanism in a frantic manner which was equalled only by the sadism of the doctors who touched, whipped, tied and burnt them without being able to restrain their desire. 'The whip made her sort of dazed, more sly, more perverse, nastier. She was then placed under continual supervision and, despite that, she succeeded in satisfying herself in a thousand and one ways... We had to resort to the strait-jacket to prevent that child from continually touching herself...but the pubic belt, the strait-jacket, the straps, the shackles, the most assiduous supervision only resulted in making her invent new means drawn from cunning and sophistication. Only cauterization with a red-hot iron gave satisfactory results... We thus believe that, in cases similar to those submitted for our observation, one shouldn't hesitate in resorting, and early too, to the red-hot iron in order to fight little girls' clitoral or vulvar onanism.'

Uncertainty at the end of the century

At the end of the 19th century, the crusade was at its peak, but the seeds of a new way of thinking could already be felt. Here and there voices could be heard that thought differently and dared to speak about sex without guilt: the voices of Krafft-Ebing, Havelock Ellis and Sigmund Freud, though still with much hesitation. A whole century of prohibition could not be easily ignored.

Krafft-Ebing, the famous psychiatrist known for his *Psychopathie Sexuali*, which depenalized some sexual perversions, nevertheless still condemned masturbation because he saw it as the 'original disorder', responsible for all other disorders. Henry Havelock Ellis, an English doctor, founder of sexual psychology, was the inventor of the notion and term 'auto-eroticism'. At the end of the century his attitude towards masturbation was the most progressive: he viewed it as a natural act without any pathological consequence. 'We can thus see that moderate masturbation is without severe effect on sane individuals.' It was finally Freud and the first psychoanalysts who laid the foundations of a new sexual morality in a hesitant re-ordering that testified to the persistence of prejudices and the perpetuity of masturbatory prohibition. Freud described the auto-eroticism of the new-born child and set forth his psycho-sexual theory in 1905 in his *Three Essays on the Theory of Sexuality*, though he still remained hesitant on the question of masturbation. He described with precision masturbatory fantasies which, he said, are only pathological when they are perverse or incestuous. Sigmund Freud was a psychogenetician who opposed the naturalist Havelock Ellis: he thought that the fantasy preceded the impulse to act and that masturbation was the result. Onanism has harmful effects which participate in the formation of neuroses because of its infantile fixation on auto-erotic behaviour. It is this dogmatic position which made Freud imagine two types of female sexuality: one mature, adult, satisfied and vaginal; the other infantile, fixed on auto-eroticism and clitoral.

This civilized debate, which still today denounces masturbation as an infantile behaviour – which is a lesser evil – but reflects a change in mentality at the turn of the century, finds an exemplary demonstration in the famous controversy about the question of the harmful effects of masturbation which excited the founders of psychoanalysis at the Vienna Psychoanalytical Society in May and June of 1910. Freud, Adler, Rank, Federn and a few others attempted to overcome their differences on that question. For some, masturbation was still the mark, male or female, of a virile protest, for others it represented a neurotic symptom, perhaps a cause of neurasthenia. For Freud himself, masturbation was nothing else than the fantasy image of coitus. However, they parted without having really decided upon the nature of masturbation and its culpability. For a large number of psychoanalysts, masturbation still remains today an act which is, if not guilt-ridden, at least infantile.

A new era finally dawned with the 20th century; some feelings of guilt and uncertainty still remained, but people's opinions were already becoming freer and less dogmatic.

The Beauty of the Gesture

> *It is a need, and when one is not driven by that need it is always a sweet thing.*
>
> Denis DIDEROT, *D'Alembert's Dream.*

Seduction, the amorous game and sexuality are always at the forefront of literary inspiration, although with the reservation demanded or permitted by each era. It's the same for masturbation, with even more modesty, which associates itself with the personal act – in the private domain – and with the sense of the corporeal and the intimate.

The great period of debauchery began by naming the sexual 'thing', then singing about eroticism and pornography, describing bodies, describing the act and finally speaking of masturbation and scatology. This was a downfall for some, regression for others, freedom for the rest – the freedom to think about the sexual within the boundaries that they had proscribed themselves. However, literature is the most accurate reflection of the inner conscience and the morality of the times, more than any fashions, laws and taboos. Literature has always been at liberty vis-à-vis masturbation and if its even course experienced a slight deviation at the end of the 17th century – Tissot's greatest hour – it has always sung about the legitimacy and, after all, the honesty of the most natural and most necessary act in human nature.

The poems of Sappho, and the texts written in licentious Rome, provide evidence, if evidence is needed, of the function of auto-eroticism in the blossoming of the self. As Martial showed while making fun of the one he called the 'left-hand whore': '...you make use of your left-hand whore, and it – your only lover – is a slave to Venus' (IX, 41). The 12th and 13th centuries, which spoke more freely about sex left us with only a few traces of masturbation, as did the following centuries, as it was not yet the object of any condemnation. It was only mentioned in the *Cackle in the Birth Room*, a burlesque satire published in 1457, which always made of the solitary act a pleasant, if sterile, alternative to life-giving pleasure: 'If I had thought that my daughter was going to be so quick at the job, I would have left her *scratching her front* until she reached twenty four.'

Masturbation was still a substitute for the act when it could not be performed, said Brantôme: 'Thinking of her, he took upon himself to corrupt and pollute himself.' It was also a part of the preliminaries of love-making – that exquisite moment of rising desire – recommended by Ambroise Paré: 'The man must also manipulate the genitals and the nipples so that she will be roused and titillated until she is smitten by desire for the male...'

In this liberal atmosphere – often erotic, sometimes licentious – the levity of the language used never even hinted at the storm that was brewing. It was to be found in the *Satirical Collection*, those 17th century *curiosa* that dispensed wise words to whoever was willing to listen and not complain about their content. There were also numerous erotic and provocative tales mixing sex and religion, like this extract from *The Nun in her Nightdress* (sometimes also called *Venus in the Cloister*) which was published anonymously in Cologne in 1719. It was an initiatory dialogue between two nuns, Agnès and Angélique, who discussed the virtues of the solitary pleasure everyone then called 'the war of five against one,' (the five fingers and the one sexual organ). 'For the Carthusians, whose retreat is strictly ordered, seek pleasures from themselves that they can't obtain from others, and thanks to a vivid and animated war they overcome the strongest temptations of the flesh. They reiterate combat as long as the enemy puts up a resistance; they use up all their energy and name those forms of expedition the war of five against one.'

They had had enough: Tissot and his killjoy instructors put a stop to the two freest thinkers, Rousseau and Diderot. One retracted his words, the other disguised himself, and both of them compromised with the murderous morality. The time had come for a sexual revolution and it was not wise to speak out loud what many thought privately.

The most surprising testimony came from Jean-Jacques, whose confession of guilt – hesitant and almost shameful – contrasted with the scrupulous sincerity of his other confessions.

Should we put it down to that genre of intimate writings in which confessions of masturbation are often veiled, allusive, half-spoken, as in Gide, Proust, Green, while provocative and explosive as in Sade or Genet? We must observe, however, that there are few confessions of masturbation compared to the numerous erotic stories, autobiographic or fictional, which openly speak of masturbation.

As for Rousseau, I think it's reasonable to suppose that his 'false confession' can be ascribed to the repressive atmosphere of which he was one of the first symptoms and, in a way one of the precursors, being so close to Tissot both in culture and in friendship. The two of them were born of the same era, ten years apart, on the shores of Lake Geneva, one in Geneva, the other in Lausanne; both of them were brought up in the Calvinist bourgeoisie by pastors hostile to sexuality, both of them fed on feelings of sexual disgust, both discovering in their adolescence Bekker's *Onania*, which would inspire Tissot to write *Masturbation* and Rousseau to write *Émile*. Even before he read or met the 'good doctor' from Lausanne, Jean-Jacques had already made a stand against vice in *Émile*. 'If he experiences once that "dangerous supplement", he is lost. Then he will always have a tense body and a nervous soul; he will carry to the grave the saddest results of that habit, the most deadly a young man can be subjected to... If the passions of a fiery temperament become invincible, I pity you, my dear Émile.'

Émile was burnt publicly in Paris in 1762. Condemned by the Parliament of Paris, Rousseau took refuge in Geneva where he met Tissot in July of the same year. Strangely enough, the admiration was reciprocal. Let us recall Jean-Jaques' 'Very annoyed not to have known earlier the treatise *On Masturbation*', and Tissot's 'I don't have anything to condemn in your work...'. Tissot did not however appreciate everything about *Émile*.

We know about the sexual inhibition of Rousseau who always remained chaste with the one he called 'Mummy', but also of his solitary practice, regular and sustained, perhaps linked to episodes of exhibitionism, fetishism and masochistic submission. A few years later, in 1766, when he began writing his *Confessions*, Jean-Jacques obviously took into account public opinion along with the opinion of his friend, the good Doctor Tissot: 'It is not what is criminal that costs the most to say, it's what is ridiculous and shameful.' (Book I). And he confessed to his crime: 'I had just come back from Italy, not entirely as I had left, but perhaps as nobody my age came back. I have brought back my virginity, but not my innocence' (Book III). The distinction is subtle, masturbation remained between the lines: 'My anxious temperament has finally shown itself, and its first involuntary eruption gave my health alarms which depict better than anything else the innocence in which I had lived until then' (op.cit.). Rousseau had now confessed enough, he condemned and made, in some respects, an act of contrition capable of lifting all suspicion from him. He took on again that term which was his own, that 'dangerous supplement', of which he had already accused Emile. 'Soon reassured, I learned of this "dangerous supplement" which cheats on nature and saves young men like me from many disorders at the expense of their health, strength and sometimes life. That vice, which shame and shyness find so convenient, holds moreover a great attraction for vivid imaginations... Seduced by that "fatal advantage", I worked at destroying the good constitution given to me by nature...' (op.cit.) That 'vice', that 'shame', that 'fatal advantage', that 'dangerous supplement' are the hypocritical alibis of Rousseau, friend of Tissot and great masturbator, undoubtedly sincere in all his confessions...except one.

Three years later, in 1769, Denis Diderot – whose *Philosophical Thoughts* had also just been burnt, and who had recently emerged from three months imprisonment in Vincennes because of his *Letters on the Blind* – who was a man inclined to prudence nevertheless wrote a very beautiful and controversial text, *D'Alembert's Dream*. In it he dramatized Julie de Lespinasse, a very bright woman, who was the mistress and great love of his friend, d'Alembert. She took offence and asked Diderot to burn the manuscript, which he did. A few years later, at the death of the treacherous Julie, d'Alembert, whom she had made executor of her will, discovered that she had not loved him. A copy of *Dream* miraculously reappeared and the book was published in 1782. In one passage, through the character of Bordeu, Diderot expressed his opinion on masturbation, against the unanimous advice of medicine and clergy:

'Bordeu: What about solitary actions?

Mlle de Lespinasse: Yes, what?

Bordeu: Perhaps they give pleasure to the individual, and our principle is wrong, or...

Mlle de Lespinasse: What, doctor!

Bordeu: Yes, mademoiselle...it is a need, and when

one is not driven by that need it is always a sweet thing. I want people to feel well, I want it very much. Do you hear?... Because I cannot sanctify my action by the seal of usefulness, I would deprive myself of a necessary and delicious moment! One makes unnecessary sacrifices. Does the nature of the overabundant fluid matter, and its colour, and the way to get rid of it?... Nature doesn't allow anything useless, and how would I be guilty of helping it, when it calls for my help through the least ambiguous symptoms? Let's not provoke it, ever, but let us lend it a hand, occasionally. I only see foolishness and wasted pleasure in idleness and denial.'

The contrast is striking between Rousseau's 'dangerous supplement' and that 'sweet and pleasant thing' mentioned by Diderot – who gave us a vibrant speech defending natural impulses and wrote the first free discourse on masturbation. He confessed to this childhood memory: 'My father's page boys taught me some college kindnesses'.

We should not forget that, at the end of the 18th century, a light, erotic, sometimes pornographic type of literature also talked about masturbation in a very liberal manner. Mercier de Compiègne reminded us that 'It is the only way to be chaste at the convent for one cannot be chaste without *stroking one's clitoris* or *touching oneself*,' and Sade – whose long life of incarceration elevated the solitary act to the state of cult and necessity – made a true way of life out of it. An obsession with pleasure occupied the days and nights of thirty years of imprisonment, thirty years of masturbation which came back in his work in an obsessive way as the model of supreme pleasure. Certainly, it is in his very first book, *The 120 Days of Sodom*, that that obsession is the most meticulously described. 'He was jerking off. He was watching, a voluptuous sensation intoxicating him, and the excess of pleasure finally carried him entirely out of himself, his moans, his groans, his strokes, all convince me that he was reaching the very last stages of pleasure, and I was sure of it when, turning my head, I saw his tool in miniature spill a few drops of sperm in the same vase I'd just filled.' If Montaigne was the inventor of the word masturbation, the divine marquis was the creator of the substantive designating its users: 'masturbator', which no one had used before then.

The 19th century presents us with the first popular argument, the defence for masturbation: the active chastity of the convents and prisons. We should not forget that one is only prisoner of oneself: 'I still call for love... Your infamous cells/ Stifle pitilessly my burning prayer;/ And I soil my body in the memory of women' (*The Cellular Prison*). Popular literature, the anonymous song of public conscience, makes the strongest rebellion against repression: 'With my five fingers, I made a virgin/ Let's masturbate, it's the pleasure of the Gods!', 'More than once, one hand beneath your petticoat/ While with the other I pulled aside your scarf/ I caressed and masturbated your mound.' There was also the *Satirical Parnassus*, that erotic anthology of the 19th century gathered together by Poulet-Malassis: 'For the setons and the cauteries/(God) made the issue peas/ And for the solitary penis/ He made fingers.'

This counting rhyme of the five fingers was even sung by the most famous of *chansonniers*, Béranger, who, at the peak of his fame, didn't hesitate from confessing: 'To have a go at your own sex/ Did you press the other too much?/ Your hand annoys me somewhat/ You use my fingers on yourself.' Another famous humourist, Tisserand, made fun of repression by...not confessing: 'There, I'm getting hard... Oh! Don't worry...I've never had that defect...for...it makes rings around my eyes!'

Also in attendance were the servants of a less ceremonious prose, those of a pornographic persuasion, at a time when brothels flourished in industrialized Europe. 'It's fiddling/ It's gurgling/ It makes my sausage swell,' confessed L.L., one of the numerous anonymous writers produced by that century. And we mustn't forget the extremely irreverent *Dialogue between the Cunt and the Arse*: 'Everything is fantasy or whims/ In the bizarre human kind/ One fucks in cunt, in arse or thigh/ Even in the hand when needed.' Further on: 'Sensual pleasure suddenly enters me/ My throbber bounced in its cage;/ To appease it I had only my hand.' And this *Ode to Masturbation*: 'What I want to sing is solitary love/ The love one makes alone, without help/ The independent love that is masturbation.' And, finally, Mililot, one of the great popular authors, didn't forget women: 'How do they manage without men when desire takes hold of them and overwhelms them so much that, their cunt all aglow, there is no oath of allegiance, whichever way you rub it.' This review of libertine facetious writings can end with *Masturbomania*, that anonymous rude work, allegedly published in 1830 'in Jerkwell, from Wrist,

Arm Street,' which gives us the tone of the whole book in a few lines in its preface: 'I sing the incomparable pleasure of Onan, the most independent, the most philosophical of all men's pleasures. It is an inspiration, it gives life to inspiration instead of stifling it.' These masturbatory verses sing of Diogenes and Socrates, Rousseau and Mirabeau, but nothing truly everlasting.

Between sexual impulse and the compulsion to write, the literary author has already made his choice, and this orientation of his personality deeply affects his work. In this praise of intimacy, some revolutionaries cry their freedom and dare to confess to masturbation. Some even confess to being masturbated by women (Baudelaire, Gautier, Maupassant); others, chaste and timid, who don't dare to instigate an encounter, religiously cultivate abstinence (Green); others remain firm believers that the solitary act is a substitute (Rousseau, Sade); others finally, amongst men, dare to meet with another man (Genet, Jouhandeau) to delude themselves about not being alone. The very same could be said about the female authors whose masturbation, though never confessed to, is certainly and fortunately much more frequent than one imagines it to be, for it allows a greater liberty to dispose of oneself.

As with writing, masturbation is first of all a solitary activity, an individual pleasure, a sign of autonomy; that is why it comes in the form of a substitute, a rival, a complement – *supplement*, Rousseau would say – to writing.

'One is never masturbated better than by oneself,' Nerval confirmed in the beauty of his delirium but was immediately corrected by Baudelaire whose hot and mysterious nymph seems to be equally adept – 'Ah, the most potent philtres/ Are not as strong as your idleness/ And you know the caress/ That returns the dead to life'. Similarly gifted are the Sapphic women of *The Flowers of Evil* – 'Lesbos, where on hot and stifling nights/ Before their mirrors, girls with hollow eyes/ Caress their ripened bodies with sterile joy,/ And taste the fruit of their nubility.' Apollinaire didn't think twice about making the Prince in *The Debauched Hospodar* benefit when, in front of Alexine and Culculine, he 'started to masturbate them each with one hand, while they were exciting his cock', and on the Orient-Express, 'hardening like a cossack' under the rhythm of the rail track, he was manually 'relieved' by his manservant: 'Cornaboeux's fingers delicately unbuttoned the prince's trousers. They took hold of the delirious penis which on all accounts justified the famous couplet by Alphonse Allais: "The exciting vibration of trains/ slides desire into the marrow of our loins"'.

Masturbation still appears in the autobiographic plots of numerous fictional stories which are as much confessions, avowels, professions of faith, late confidences of a childhood emotion, of an everlasting pleasure. Are *Sebastien Roch* and his solitary relapses at the Jesuits not a double of Octave Mirbeau? 'Left to himself, most of the time sitting or lying down on the bed, his body inactive, he found it hard to fight against the temptations which came back in greater numbers, more precise every day, against the unleashed madness of impure images which besieged him, inflaming his imagination, whipping his flesh, pushing him into shameful relapses, immediately followed by disgust, exhaustion where his soul sunk as in death.'

Would the hero of *The Apprentice* be Raymond Guérin himself, when he questioned in his telegraphic style: 'Perhaps men and women had more pleasure alone than together. Why didn't they have the courage of their convictions?'; and when he confessed: 'To masturbate was not very original... He was under the impression that if he was confessing, he would be thought of as disgusting... All he could have done was to fight this solitary fondness. But why? In the name of what? Religion? The fear of being damned? He didn't believe in it any longer. And even when he still believed a little, until around fifteen, sixteen, it hadn't stopped him. On the contrary, it only exacerbated his desires. So? Morals? No, he would not deprive himself of a pleasure which exceeded all others, in the name of morality.' Guérin asked the intimate questions one formulates for oneself, those about the equivalence of the 'supplement', about the impossible confession and about repression. Why repress this pleasure, he says, which exceeds all others? And if all men and all women were having more pleasure alone than together, silence and interdict would then have the merit, or the function, to silence that subversive confession. Here are new arguments to offer the censors: avoid the confidences, forbid the revelation of this subversive pleasure, for fear of contamination!

Masturbation can now be found in slang – in Céline, Boudard, Le Breton and also in Roth and Bukowski in American Literature. In Alphonse Boudard's *The Hospital* – which carries, appropriately, the subtitle *A Hospitobiographism* – one of the patients, Michel

Félonian, cannot restrain 'his disgraceful habit,' 'takes hold of his cock again...gives it a good pasting...not just a casual jerk-off, he chokes the Populace the whole night long, Félonian.' Boudard *hospitobiographises* himself and is certainly talking about himself when, by way of defence, he hurls at the reader: 'To the man who has never polished his own cock may the first spittoon be thrown.'

Parisian slang developed its largest range under the pen of Auguste Le Breton, who repeated commonplaces about masturbation, but in an almost foreign language. 'Staring at the little shrimp and her ringed lamps, I guessed she had played the mandolin all night.' And further: 'As soon as she had turned off the light, he masturbated, imagining her in the buff.' The language is short, concise, but efficient, as if all these words, non-existent in the usual register, take on a meaning thanks to their context only, and to the suggestive power of their images.

Charles Bukowski is a different style altogether and his *Notes of a Dirty Old Man* appears like the testimony of a contemporary libertine freed from sexual taboos, which some call fantasy and others perversion. 'he came out and made the phone. he found that by taking out the mouthpiece he could slip his penis into the phone. he slid it back and forth and it felt good. very good. soon he completed his act, hung up the phone, zipped up and sat down across from Jack.' Sex is an everyday consumer product.

In a similar vein, Philip Roth is as direct and obscene in *Portnoy's Complaint*, confessing to the repeated crime of food masturbation with the help of a 'big purplish piece of raw liver' his mother had left in the refrigerator. 'My first piece I had in the privacy of my own home, rolled round my cock in the bathroom at three-thirty.' The crime is admitted, the worst thing he had ever done: 'I fucked my own family's dinner.' This provocative confession may be seen as a reaction against the puritan activism which was still very influential in the United States.

Female masturbatory love, solitary or sapphic, has recently found its literary expression with more difficulty than the male confession, partly because of a certain reticence on the part of publishers. The mutual caresses in Violette Leduc's *Therese and Isabelle*, which the publisher had asked to be removed in 1964 was published two years later, testifying to an evolution in morality: 'The rubbing to and fro was no servitude but the rubbing of beatitude. I was losing myself in Isabelle's finger as she was losing herself in mine. How it dreamt, our conscientious finger... What marriages of movements! Clouds helped us. We were resplendent with light.' Here the words of love are of an entirely different tone, the hand is female, the writing that of a woman; there are no trouser flies or any sperm, the imagery here is of the scent of beatitude, movement, cloud, light. Female masturbation exists in another world, inaccessible to men, and opens onto a world of sensual delights. Under a provocative title *If Pigs Could Fly*, Rocco and Antonia give another testimony: 'And she told me we could do what we do when we are alone. She began to masturbate, her hand resting on her pubis, her finger stretched as she burrowed in. So I lay on my back and did the same. She opened her eyes, turned her head slightly and still caressing herself, looked at me. I stopped, ashamed, and laughed, but I could have cried with shame...'

Shame, which we call decency when we talk about sex, is a product of shyness, whose function is most certainly to protect oneself from the impudence of seduction, but which then inhibits so many sexual impulses that it dries up desire. The liberation of morality is surely nothing else than the absence of the feeling of shame with the partner one has chosen, or with oneself.

A descriptive and commercial kind of erotic prose, destined for feeble imaginations or literary masturbators, has appeared in recent years. One of its leading exponents is Emmanuelle Arsan, undoubtedly the autobiographical author – at least in fantasy – of *Emmanuelle,* who exists not to forbid herself anything and so enables other women to live vicariously through her and do the things which they don't allow themselves to do: 'Emmanuelle's flesh trembled. Her legs parted and she raised her pubis slightly, offering herself with a movement of inimitable gracefulness, stretching the lips of her sex as for a child's kiss... She arched up, moaned for a few minutes. Her hands continued their task on the sensitive tips of her breast until her orgasm subsided, calmed, leaving her inert and lifeless.'

Very different is this great work of literature which barely brushes against reality; allusive, suggestive, impressionist, it proceeds by touching the imaginary. It is the writing of desire, true eroticism: Zola's description of *Nana,* where nothing is said, and yet everything is said: 'Nana was absorbed in her own rapture... A thrill of tenderness seemed to have passed through her limbs. Her eyes wet, she made herself smaller, the better to feel herself. Then she unclenched her hands, lowered them with a sliding motion alongside herself as far as her loins, which she tightly gripped in a nervous grasp. And, throwing out her chest, melting in a caress of her whole body, she rubbed her cheeks on the right, the left, against her shoulders in a fondling manner. Her greedy mouth breathed desire on her. She stretched her lips, kissed herself longingly under the armpit, laughing at the other Nana, also kissing herself in the mirror.'

This play on the double is the living reflection of masturbation, the praise of narcissism, the cultivation of solitary pleasure, the natural homosexuality in the mirror image that the identical other reflects, who is the only one to understand: 'Why I have become a lesbian, O Bilitis, you ask?... You, who are a woman, you know how I feel. You do it as you do it for yourself.' In this long ode to homonymous desire, *The Songs of Bilitis*, the great libertine Pierre Louÿs denounced the difference between the sexes by underlining each person's propensity to find another self. Thus the fundamental importance of auto-eroticism in *sexuality* is better understood, for sexuality always means *two*. 'How pretty you are with your arms raised, your curved back and your rosy breasts... Your body folds on itself like a scarf, you caress your skin which shivers and sensual delight inundates your enraptured eyes...you almost undulate, lying down to the rhythm of your memories.'

For me, a Titian painting appeared beneath Louÿs's pen. I see it now in the Uffizi Gallery: the *Venus of Urbino* caressing her body and trembling with desire, her hand placed on her sex, curved, nestled and penetrating – our ancestors would have said '*pudendum mulieri*'; 'caught in the act', I would add. It is quite surprising to notice how much one of Modigliani's reclining nudes resembles it: same attitude, same lascivious reclining pose, same curls of hair flowing onto the same shoulder, same position of the arm on the belly and the hand on the sex, more suggestive even, for, by his time, there was no need to hide anything. Only the face is different, fleshy in Titian, elongated in Modigliani. It is undoubtedly an allusive replica which shows, as if there was a need, the continuity of the *beauty of the gesture*.

Confessing to masturbation is a high-flying exercise which few have tried their hands at. And when they have attempted it, it has always been in a summary way, as a veiled allusion, or a guilty memory, rarely with a clear and strong voice, except for the provocative voice of the Onan afficionados who elevated onanism into an art of living close to a cult of the self. Despite his profession of faith: 'I commanded myself to dare to say everything I dare to do, and I do not appreciate thoughts considered unpublishable...', Montaigne the precursor confessed nothing. Then it was the turn of Rousseau, the great masturbator before the Eternal One, who swore to the heavens to tell the whole truth and who shamefully delivered just a few touchings. Let's remember Diderot, Sade, and Nerval, who were more honest, but let's also admit that it is never easy to confess the most intimate secrets of one's being.

'Besides, I know the harm I'm doing to myself in telling this and what will follow,' Gide confessed. 'I foresee the advantage one could have against me. But my story is only worth telling if it's true. Let's say that I'm writing it as penance.' Does the 'confessional' genre have a limit? 'Real scenes,' Louÿs continued, 'are more difficult to recount than inventions, for the logic of life is less clear than that of a story.' The truth is first and foremost in childhood, and all our witnesses confess their first experience: 'The door opens,' Aragon humbly confessed in *Paris Peasant*, 'and dressed in her stockings only, the one I chose moves forward, simpering… Let happy people cast the first stone: they don't need this atmosphere where I find myself, younger, amidst the disruptions that have incessantly thinned my existence, with the memory of *old habits* whose traces and tracks still hold much power over my heart.' A life event is deeply affecting only because it reminds us of another we cannot forget. For Aragon, his first woman reminds him of his first habits and their guilty aftertaste which prevent him from forgetting, as the first erections, with Leiris, remind him of the morbid sensations he had to be cured of. He remembered them in *Manhood*: 'I'm incapable of distinguishing in my first erections that unhealthy turgidity, and I think that at the beginning the erection scared me, for I mistook it for the offensive return of the illness. Of course, my illness had given me some pleasure, because of the hypersensitivity it gave me, but I knew it was something bad and abnormal because I was being treated for it.'

Pain, pleasure, shame and guilt are often mixed up with first sexual experiences to sully the course of a whole life. This first meeting is thus marked with the seal of pleasure or a deep traumatism. In his admirable *Autobiography*, Julian Green showed his innocence when, in bed at seven o'clock with the door to his room open, his mother was keeping an eye on him, 'having for some faults a horror I only knew her to have... I was innocence personified and remained like that for a long time, but it's a fact that, lying on my back, in my bed, I took pleasure exploring with my hand this body that I was barely conscious of as another part of myself. How old was I then? Five perhaps.'

But one evening his sister, Mary, in charge of keeping an eye on him, caught him – 'Why should I have hidden, when I didn't feel guilty?' – and in one movement pulled back the cover and called their mother. He appeared as he was, 'hands in the forbidden area'. '*I'll cut it off!*' his mother screamed, brandishing a bread knife. It was only later, with the reminder of the memory and understanding the English by then, that Green realized the full implication, a late symptom of the age-long persecution. This reminder of the forbidden and the supreme punishment is present in every page of his *Journal* like a leitmotiv of chastity: 'My God, what a strange cross is the flesh!', and with a constant play between impulse and counter-impulse: 'I want to start reading the Bible again every night, like I used to, even if that reading is a weak help against temptations,' (6th October, 1928). 'There are thoughts of the flesh that give vertigo,' (29th January, 1929).

The confession is made in one stroke on the very first page of *If it die*... Still a child, Gide is playing with the caretaker's son under the big table in the dining room: 'What are you doing down there?' the maidservant asked them. 'Nothing, we are playing,' they answered in unison. 'And we noisily shook some toys we had brought for that purpose. In reality we were having fun in a different way – one next to the other, but not one with the other. However, we had what I knew later were called "bad habits".'

Proust too is sparing with details in his published work, but talks about masturbation more openly in the correspondence of his youth: 'My dear little grandad, I am asking from your kindness the sum of thirteen francs that I wanted to ask from Monsieur Nathan but that mother prefers me to ask of you. This is why. I really need to see a woman in order to put a stop to my bad habits of masturbation...' (18th May, 1888). He indulged himself with assiduity, however. One can find a trace of it in the first pages of *Swann's Way*: 'I climbed sobbing to the very top of the house, next to the study room, under the roofs, in a little room smelling of irises... Destined to a more special and common use, that room, from where one could see during the day as far as the donjon of Roussainville-le-Pin, was used for a long time as a shelter by me, undoubtedly because it it was the only room I was allowed to lock myself in, a shelter for those of my pursuits requiring an inviolable solitude: reading, daydreaming, tears and sensual delight.' Sex and writing are still mixed in this retreat from the world required by privacy, far away even from an attentive mother and the spectre of a father, there where the little Marcel can create his own world.

With Maurice Sachs, sex is beautiful, free, blossoming. No censor beside him, no persecutor, the first excitement of *Sabbat* is perceived as a first happiness. 'In the boarding school in Luza, where I had been sent, I started to grow smarter. Before going to sleep, I had the habit of storing safely a wallet made from calf which was my treasured possession. I don't know how I happened to start rubbing it against my body, but the wallet was soon between my thighs. I carried on rubbing it there and before long the most vivid pain contracted my whole body, a light foam dampened the sheet and my body happy, stupefied and softened, relaxed suddenly. The first sexual delight deserves to stay eternally in our memories, for it is, though hazardous and naïve, the promise of human continuity and its craziest extravagances.' Freud would have enjoyed himself with all these symbols: sex and money, making love with a wallet found 'I don't know how', 'between my thighs'! Sachs humbly admits to it. It was his treasured possession and it gave him his first sensual pleasure. There is a happiness and a profound authenticity in this confession of youth which sounds like a marvellous memory and contrasts with Rousseau's guilty sex or Green's torment of chastity. Maurice Sachs continues as he remembers his 'summer pleasures' when at the age of thirteen, wanting to unite with nature, he often made love to the earth, 'alone, arms outstretched as if crucified, sex thrust deep into the coolness of the trampled earth, wonderfully lost.' Love with oneself is not only this filthy stain we were presented with, it is more certainly a sumptuous inner meeting which doesn't exclude any of the other modes of sexuality and, on the contrary, gives them an inaccessible freedom. Leiris confirms this communion of oneself with the cosmos in this passage in Aurora. 'I embraced the earth with my outstretched arms and it was really the whole world with its procession of laws and cardinal points that I possessed then...'

Let us take *Moravagine* as Blaise Cendrars' personal and intimate testimony, for he was eager to describe how he had written this incredible fiction. Like Sade or Genet, Moravagine-Cendrars spent years in a cell, at the bottom of a stinking hole, first in Presbourg, then in the same cell as the Iron Mask: 'I caressed myself till it bled,' he confessed, 'thinking I would die of exhaustion. Then it became a habit, a mania, an exercise, a game, a kind of hygiene, a relief. I was doing it several times a day, mechanically, without thinking about it, indifferent, cold. And that gave me some toughness. I was now more solid, more robust. I had a healthy appetite. I started to put on weight.' With all due respect to the ever vigilant censors and, at the risk of making Tissot turn in his grave, masturbation possesses many virtues, Cendrars seems to tell us. It is a powerful tonic, it is a Fountain of Youth, it is a sign of life and health.

Michel Tournier, who openly made his confession in *The Meteors*, entitled it 'On masturbation' and immediately placed this question in its proper field, the imaginary. 'The brain provides the sexual organ with an imaginary object. This object rests with the hand to embody it.' The hand is thus the ideal partner. Like an actor, the hand plays the role it is given. It is, he says, a calculator for the primitive, an alphabet for the deaf-mute, 'but its masterpiece is masturbation. There it becomes at will either penis or vagina.' How many notice that this part of our body, the sexual organ, falls within the scope of the hand? It is within its reach, within its dimensions, like a tool for a good craftsman. It looks like it was made for that.

There are many more testimonies about the importance, the interest, the attraction exercised by masturbation – witnesses for the defence, if I may say so – after the long indictment of the Public Prosecutor. Amongst those I will just recall the 'beautiful words' of Guillaume Fabert in his *Self-portrait as an Erection*, for he pleads with sincerity and one recognizes in him the accents of truth. Not everybody is able to make such confessions openly. Fabert has the right and free tone of the pioneers of the inaccessible: 'For more than thirty years I've been masturbating steadfastly a few times a week, and I feel no physical ailments nor moral disorders.' Fabert argues that masturbation has so many virtues – it relaxes, it comforts, it animates body and soul, it heals sexual failure as well as momentary blues, 'It is to sex what aspirin is to medicine: *panacea*.' Fabert is happy in an unalterable ritual that enriches and participates deeply in his love life, but which is in no way a subordinate activity. He makes it a profession of faith: 'I willingly admit, to whomever asks me, that I am an earnest, persevering and happy masturbator.'

Finally we have the devotees of the cult of masturbation – inspired by homosexuality – in whom one finds the male obsession with the genitals and often the illusion of sexuality in pairs. Genet says it well in *Our Lady of the Flowers*: 'Lucky for me to raise egoistic masturbation to the dignity of a cult! As soon as I start, a filthy and supernatural transposition shifts the truth. Everything in me becomes a worshipper.' Contemplation in desire isolates the masturbator from the rest of the world, the sex-god appears to him, the body is his temple but the communion is only with himself. Prison life imposes many restraints and even the solitary embrace has to be furtive: 'My hatred and my horror of this revenge made me harden even more, for I felt under my fingers my penis stiffening – and I shook it until finally...without taking my eyes off the warden...' Genet, who felt no reluctance in staging sex scenes and mixing bodies, admits the deep, intimate dimension of all sexuality: one only makes love with oneself.

Sartre drove a barbed dart into Jouhandeau's back in his virulent *Saint Genet, Actor and Martyr*. 'I say it straight: these dialectics stink. Firstly, they exaggerate the importance of a few solitary or shared masturbations. Big deal. What is the heinous crime? Between gay men, human relationships are as possible as between a man and a woman.' Then, Sartre goes on, one has to be very vain to imagine one has committed 'the sin which incurs damnation'. So he condemns Jouhandeau, who would like to offer himself as a victim and in that way regain a good clear conscience. But it is not he, Sartre, who would make such a confession. We have to admit that the child Marcel in *Ways of Adolescence* expresses in a very beautiful language the contours of sensual pleasure: 'Pure spirit some months, body forgotten, abandoned. Then found again, faithful animal, panting, attentive, without a grudge, always ready to please.'

Let's close this record of the 'beauty of the gesture' with Vincent Ravalec's latest provocation, his *Portrait of Men who Masturbate*, sub-titled 'The Masturbators', a small bilingual booklet illustrated with photographs of the offensive object, destined for drivers curious of initiatory rituals or lost in the night between the hippodrome and the Bois de Boulogne. The discourse is dry, direct, efficient, in each line hands meet sexual organs in a debauchery of pleasure and excitement, words meet words – 'dick', 'member', 'thingamy', 'tool', 'come', 'bisexual', 'hair' – stallions at the paroxysm of desire meet other stallions looking for pleasure, men, a few women to excite the hard-on, and then the god Pan, called here 'member', 'dick', 'cock', 'lust'... 'There, it used to be special to show one's cock every night; cars would stop and watch them wanking like idiots...' This collective outburst certainly has the merit of creating the excitement which some males lack. As with every paroxysm, sex has its limits and each of us feels its impending necessity: 'You know, there are so many nights to come that sometimes I have vertigo. If we were condemned to live two thousand years, do you think we would still come here, or wouldn't it have an effect on us any longer?'

Postlude

I have come round to thinking that masturbation is the only great habit, the primitive need.

Sigmund Freud, *Letter to Fliess*, 1897.

For the majority of us, masturbation is the most widespread sexual practice, alone or in pairs; for the majority it has been their first sexual experience; for the majority, finally, it is the guarantee of personal balance and growth within a couple; for everyone it is almost surely the most fundamental element of sexuality – essential to its maturing, to its full realization as well as its perpetuity. It remains, however, the most solid taboo of our western sexual morality.

Years have passed, the storm has abated, masturbation now has a voice. And yet, it is still not sufficiently exculpated and we need to reaffirm quite clearly that every interdict is today lifted. It is permissible and normal. It is beautiful, good, nice, agreeable, decent, simple, excellent, acceptable, laudable, deserving, useful, worthy, happy, frequent, regular, common, understandable, appetizing, attractive, captivating, amusing, interesting, stimulating, strengthening, thrilling, revivifying, cheering, quickening, comforting, invigorating, exciting, moving, intoxicating, voluptuous, legitimate, reasonable, defensible, excusable, permitted, legal, authorized, loyal, right, valid, justified, correct, fair, legitimate, honest, proper, natural...to masturbate, whether we are a man or a woman, and especially if we are a woman, for it is still far too frequent that women and young girls – but very rare for men – do not dare to surrender themselves to auto-eroticism, though it would do them much good.

The great drama of masturbation comes from the fact that we don't talk about it. It is not of course a question of talking about oneself, of confessing, of admitting to one's own practice or intimacy – the inquisition has ended – but it is now acceptable to talk about masturbation, its nature, its functions, its role in individual life and in the role of a couple. As with everything sexual, if we don't discuss it, that's because of its so-called 'natural' character. And it is for that same reason that there is no – or so little – sex education, for why learn about what is considered so natural!

The understanding of human sexuality is, after all, quite recent; it has only evolved over the last few decades. As for auto-eroticism and masturbation, opinions were first hesitant with the great pioneers of sexuality – Ellis, Freud, Kinsey, Masters and Johnson, Shere Hite – then reserved, because of the silence of psychoanalysis on that subject. Today a clear and coherent opinion is expressed by all the practitioners of sexology.

Masturbation is a manual technique designed to provide an orgasm, alone or as a couple, individually or reciprocally. As a prototype of sexuality, it has allowed countless scientific and technical discoveries, which is not the least of its paradoxes: the first discovery by Leeuwenhoek, which triggered the great persecution we've been through, was of course the result of masturbation, for how else could he obtain spermatozoa? The very important work of Masters and Johnson, who showed the physiological reality of human sexuality, and in particular that of the female, was only possible through the observation of several thousand orgasms, reached by masturbation. And, finally, fertilization *in vitro*, the remarkable treatment for some cases of sterility, also uses sperm obtained by masturbation.

As a primary experience, masturbation structures nascent sexuality. It proceeds from a predetermined impulse which encourages the exploration and the awakening of sensory perception. Already *in utero*, and well before its system is mature, the foetus explores its own surroundings and strokes its own body. Auto-stimulation is in this period a very frequent activity and it has not been ruled out that the foetus already experiences orgasms in its mother's womb.

The new-born baby's sensory education continues; the mother's hands meticulously caress the baby's body, except for the sexual organ. It is this area which the baby itself will touch in order to learn all its reactions. The *sensorial birth* of the sexual organ happens very naturally, simply by the hand, whose touch gives rise to sensations which arouse this area from the first days of life. Kinsey observed that with infants less than a year old there were some touchings and an active masturbation from the first months, the first orgasm at only five months! 'In a baby or young male,' he added, 'orgasm is the exact replica of the adult orgasm, except for the absence of ejaculation.'

The sexual organ exists because it is stroked, because it is stimulated, manipulated in early infancy, and because it provides different sensations than the rest of the body – those which we call *pleasure*. Once he or she has discovered the agreeable sensations that this manipulation of the genitals provides, the little boy or little girl can continue the practice throughout their life with varying frequency, according to their age and their manner of sexual relationships. Masturbation is neither dirty, nor shameful, nor perverse, nor reserved for adolescence, nor for celibacy. It is a necessary and indispensable stage of maturing and the guarantee of a couple's sexual autonomy.

This first sequence of auto-eroticism and sexual play is followed by a second at puberty to reaffirm the choice of impulses. Masturbation is used then to win over one's own reactions before living them out with a partner. Moral attitudes have often repressed infantile masturbation with an energetic 'Don't touch, it's dirty!', condemning to neglect and oblivion this area of the body that is now heavily charged with fear and bewilderment. It is often enough to generate deep inhibitions. If children practice masturbation publicly and without restraint, it is important not to reprimand them, which will have the consequence of making them feel guilty, and also inhibiting them in their future sexuality. It is better to talk quietly about propriety while remaining permissive of a behaviour which is fundamentally 'good', for it belongs to them and can be practised privately. This childhood auto-eroticism helps to ease inner tensions and to reassure a worried child. It is certainly a good anxiety relief, in no way harmful or depraved.

Viewed in this light, masturbation appears as a prototype of sexuality, as a fundamental primary experience, as a necessary stage of maturity and even as a therapeutic tool allowing women, for example, to learn the vaginal amplification of clitoral pleasure and men to better know and control the ejaculatory reflex. It is practised alone or in pairs, it is one of the variants of love and a complement to coitus. It is not a mere substitute, but an indispensable part of mutual growth which, however, seems very different among men, for whom it appears rather stereotyped, and women, for whom it varies *ad infinitum*. The man who stimulates himself has a constant tendency to concentrate on the sensations of his genital area by moving his hand, pseudo-vagina, up and down on his penis. Women who masturbate use the most varied methods. Masters and Johnson noted that amongst their volunteers, there were not two women who touched themselves in the same way. The majority stroked the clitoris or rather stimulated all the area of the *mons Veneris*, with their hand or an artifice, a sheet or a piece of clothing, in a simple stroke, a circular movement or else a slight rubbing; others were pulling at the labia minora or moving a finger in the vagina; others still were using a contraction of the thighs, a movement of the pelvis, caresses of the whole body or stimulation of the breasts. Both men and women however use fantasy, imaginary scenes, erotic memory, or some props for the imagination – books, photos or videos, although the main difference between men and women is certainly the very surprising fact that some women can reach orgasm through the lone act of imagination.

This recent discovery is not short of being subversive for the defenders of order and repression who have never totally disappeared. It is, for example, very surprising to read even today warnings coming from doctors who claim to know about sexuality. A certain Professor Joyeux, for example, holds such views: 'One can present masturbation (to the boy) as a waste of energy, as a waste of semen which represents a withdrawal...' Or, again, from the same author: 'But generally female masturbation increases anxiety and destabilizes...and can lead to self-loathing when there is a feeling of guilt.' One could say the same about ideas of immaturity which sometimes remain linked to masturbation and which seems to me a disguised form of discrimination. In opposition to sexual reality, which shows that the majority of men and women practice auto or hetero-masturbation, the widespread notion that masturbation is the sign of an infantile immaturity derives from the Freudian theory, now discredited, that masturbation comes from an immature pregenital impulse, as opposed to the mature, adult, genital sexuality which seeks vaginal coitus to the exclusion of manual practices. It is this same idea which had Freud – not a great expert on sexuality, he admitted with regret – imagining that two female categories coexisted; immature clitoral women giving themselves pleasure through masturbation and vaginal adult women taking part in complete intercourse: a male and phallocratic view, in a way privileging genital pleasure. We know that to be entirely otherwise. Masters and Johnston have clearly shown the physiological equivalence of these two so-called types of orgasm, and one would confirm today that there are some women who are not receptive to themselves and others who are, some women who prefer fantasies and others who prefer an actual presence, and that one often observes a competition between the potential sources of pleasure, whether clitoral or vaginal. Masturbatory pleasure is not the lesser, it is just different.

However, a certain level of confusion about masturbation still remains. There are still a number of manuals of psychiatry and even sexology which express a reservation concerning the too frequent or prolonged practice of masturbation beyond adolescence. It is fundamental to acknowledge that no link between illness and masturbation has ever been shown; on the contrary, the positive effects have been better understood. The very rare men who have never experienced masturbation are generally deeply inhibited and repressed. Most women who have a happy sexuality know and practice masturbation while, amongst those who have sexual problems, the majority have never had access to it.

The habit of masturbation practised throughout a lifetime is a guarantee of personal fulfillment. It is also beneficial for a couple in that it acts as a buffer between two partners, their different sensibilities, their desires and their pleasures.

How many couples have failed due to lack of

combatants because they didn't know or forbade themselves those acts of auto-eroticism which could have helped them to survive a difficult period? How many couples have self-destructed as a result of the clumsiness or inexperience of one of them, and because the other one – by not allowing themselves any masturbatory activity – was not able to bypass that instance of their partner's inadequacy and de-dramatize the situation? How many men live with the permanent frustration of repressed eroticism with a partner without desire, because they forbid themselves – or someone else forbids them – the royal path of autonomy? How many women will never know the pleasure they have dreamt so much about – and have idealized – because they imagine it can only come from someone else? And how many people still live unhappily, either by themselves or with their partners, without realizing that personal fulfillment is the most certain guarantee of a couple's stability?

In order that those who believe that I only see the 'physical side' of sex are no longer deceived, I would like to ensure that it is very clear that I do not speak only about the superficialities of the body – the only concrete reality of love – but as much about love's emotional aspects and about the 'symbols' of which it is composed. This rhetoric is anything but a re-iteration. Because sex has been kept in a kind of symbolic utopia – not so long ago Lacanian theories seemed to say that there was no man, there was no woman and there was no body – I now want to speak about the reality. A reality which surpasses inner conflict by understanding the landmarks of emotional life, a reality which is sometimes self-supporting and which can evolve through better self-knowledge, or a discovery of an often non-existent eroticism. This is in opposition to one part – monolithic and initiator of anathemas – of psychoanalysis which has always supported only the symbolic nature of every sexual disorder. I am not talking about theory here, but about the totalitarian use to which language has been put. The sexologic experience was different; it showed that the disappearance of the symptom was not followed by a cataclysm and that, on the contrary, it allowed an 'improved condition' of oneself and the other, sometimes at the cost of personal labour. Masturbation, which is one of the means of this improvement, allows the couple to grow in confidence again. It allows the woman to escape an unsatisfactory sex-life for a while and enables her to learn or to re-learn the sensations of her most intimate self. It is a therapeutic tool which can help her to achieve a sense of fulfillment, but it is in no way a panacea.

In a very short space of time we have moved on from Rousseau's 'dangerous supplement' and the 'cynical expedient' of the doctors of the 19th century, to imagine today the definite positive value of this 'gesture of love' which gives pleasure and arouses eroticism, without any profound change in mentalities.

May *In Praise of Masturbation* liberate consciences and appease minds for – and Montaigne would not have denied this – masturbation is undoubtedly the true worth of our gestures of love.

References

References to the contemporary literature cited in the text, where the reader can check to ascertain the complete context. First (English language) editions referenced if possible, though most have been followed by other editions.

Apollinaire, G., *The Debauched Hospodar*, Paris, Olympia Press, 1953.

Aragon, L., *Paris Peasant*, London, Cape, 1971.

Arsan, E., *Emmanuelle*, New York, Grove Press, 1971.

Boudard, A., *l'Hôpital, une Hostobiographie*, Paris, La Table ronde, 1972.

Bukowski, C., *Notes of a Dirty Old Man*, San Francisco, City Lights, 1981.

Céline, L.-F., *Journey to the End of the Night*, London, Chatto & Windus, 1934.

Cendrars, B., *Moravagine*, London, Penguin, 1979.

Fabert, G., *Autoportrait en Érection*, Paris, Régine Deforges, 1989.

Genet, J., *Our Lady of the Flowers*, London, Anthony Blond, 1964.

Gide, A., *If it die*, London, Secker & Warburg, 1950.

Green, J., *Autobiography*, London, Marion Boyars, 1993.

Guérin, R., *l'Apprenti*, Paris, Gallimard, 1981.

Leduc, V., *Therese and Isabelle*, New York, Farrar, Straus & Giroux, 1967.

Leiris, M., *Aurora*, London, Atlas, 1990.

Leiris M, *Manhood*, New York, Grossman, 1963.

Mirbeau, O., *Sebastien Roch*, Sawtry, Dedalus, 1998.

Proust, M., *Swann's Way*, London. Chatto &

Windus, 1929.
Ravalec, V., *The Masturbators*, Paris, Le Dernier terrain vague, 1995.
Rocco et Antonia, *Si les porcs avaient des ailes*, Paris, Stock, 1977.
Sachs, M., *Witches' Sabbath*, London, Cape, 1965.
Sartre, J-P., *Saint Genet*, New York, Georges Braziller, 1963.
Tournier, M., *Gemini*, London, Collins, 1981.

Small glossary of masturbation

Here is a non-exhaustive inventory of derivatives, synonyms and qualifiers of masturbation gathered from more than a hundred books dealing with this 'odious perversion'. The passionate outburst of the enemies of masturbation never had words strong enough to name this 'supreme evil' and always used different names. The function of this impressive and quite incongruous catalogue was obviously to provoke anxiety, shame and guilt. However, one will notice a few great signatures in this unprecedented catalogue, like Rousseau's 'dangerous supplement' and 'fatal advantage', Diderot's 'the sweet thing' and 'the delicious moment', Freud's 'primitive need', but also Sartre's 'the pure demonic act'. This spectacular list of nearly eight hundred synonyms can be compared to the inventory of Pierre Guiraud's sexual semiology which records one thousand three hundred words to designate the penis, and prompts us to think that, in the context of its repression and the grand epoch of the doctors of love, masturbation was certainly the first language referent.

abject crime
abject disease
abnormal behaviour
abnormal fixation
abominable crime
abominable infamy
abominable madness
abominable practice
abomination
absolute irresponsibility
abuse of oneself
abusive act
abusive jouissance
abusive practice
abusive request
accidental gesture

accidental rubbing
accidental weakness
act against nature
act of aggression
act of the hand
amorous convulsion
amorous learning
amorous subterfuge
ancestral defect
ancient habit
animal crime
animal regression
anticipating substitute
antiphysical act
antiphysical crime
appearance of appearance
appeasing manoeuvre
artificial infamy
artificial lust
artificial means
artificial sensual pleasure
artificial vice
atrocious vice
auto-complacency
auto-erotic activity
auto-erotic ipsation
auto-erotic satisfaction
auto-eroticism
auto-manipulation
automatic reflex
auto-pollution
auto-satisfaction
auto-sexuality
auto-stimulation
auto-sufficiency
bad act
bad desire
bad habit
bad manoeuvre
banal behaviour
barbarious process
barren gesture
biological reality
biological request
bitter delight
bizarre practice
bogus need
cancer
caress
catastrophic error
cause for madness
celibate mania
censored crime
childish compromise
childish diversion
childish enuresis
childish nonsense
childish passivity
childish play
childish stain
childish vice
chiromania
chronic demented practice
clandestine pleasure

cleansing habit
cleansing manoeuvre
cleansing pollution
clitoral stain
clitorization
coitus interrupted
coitus interruptus
college kindness
common gesture
common vice
compensation mania
compensatory gesture
compensatory pleasure
complete disorder
compulsive act
concrete error
constitutional aberration
contra naturam
contra-nature discharge
contra-sexuality
convenient satisfaction
convenient vice
corrupt depravity
corrupted imagination
corruption
corruption of morals
crime
crime against God
crime against humanity
crime before God
crime of Onan
criminal caress
criminal habit
criminal neurosis
criminal passion
criminal pleasure
criminal practice
criminal sensual pleasure
criminal sex
criminal trade
crisis of desire
cursed sin
cynical expedient
dangerous discharge
dangerous failure
dangerous leaning
dangerous recreation
dangerous supplement
deadly disease
deadly habit
death peril
debauched trade
debauchery
debauchery against nature
decadence
deceitful jouissance
deceitful libertinage
deception of nature
deception of the absence
deceptive pleasure
decongestive eroticism
deed of darkness
degeneration
delicious moment

delicious practice
demonic act
deplorable habit
deplorable laxity
depraved act
depraved allurement
depraved complacency
depraved epidemic
depraved excitement
depraved fatigue
depraved friction
depraved habit
depraved manoeuvre
depraved narcissism
depraved play
depraved rubbing
depraved stain
depraved touching
depravity
detrimental habit
deviant behaviour
deviation
diabolic pleasure
didactic experience
digital dexterity
digital manoeuvre
digital touching
dirty gesture
dirty habit
dirty obsession
dirty sensual delight
disappointing experience
disastrous mania
disastrous overwork
discharge instinct
discharging conduct
disgraceful habit
disgusting depravity
disgusting infamy
disgusting picture
dishonest touching
disordered pleasure
disorderly use
dissolute morals
distressing spectacle
disturbing habit
dorsal consumption
drug addition
education vice
effusion of life
egocentrism
emotional imperfection
enormity
enormity of the hand
episodic practice
episodic weakness
erotic satisfaction
essential stage
excess of debauchery
excessive discharge
excessive excretion
excessive jouissance
exploration of oneself
extra-genital ideal

fallacious abstinence
false convulsion
false delight
false jouissance
false need
false-coitus
family drama
fascinating delight
fatal advantage
fatal attraction
fatal career
fatal deception
fatal depravity
fatal disorder
fatal excess
fatal habit
fatal instinct
fatal lapse
fatal leaning
fatal mania
fatal manoeuvre
fatal onanism
fatal passion
fatal practice
fatal secret
fatal vice
fault contrary to nature
faux-pas
filthy habit
filthy stain
filthy thought
first experience
first sensual pleasure
fixed idea
fleeting pleasure
flight of the imagination
forbidden leakage
forbidden venture
forced excretion
forced pleasure
formidable scourge
fornication
fornicatory substitute
fortuitous jerking-off
frantic debauchery
frantic leaning
frantic onanism
frenzied practice
frenzy
fretwork
fruitless work
fundamental element
furtive jouissance
genetic fraud
genital artifice
genital ersatz
genital excess
genital irritation
genital misadventure
genital play
genital pleasure
genital prostitution
genital pseudo-reflex
genital vice

gesture
gesture of love
ghastly crime
gracious movement
great habit
guilt attempt
guilt manifestation
guilt orgasm
guilt stain
guilt substitute
guilty blindness
guilty carelessness
guilty caresses
guilty conduct
guilty derangement
guilty epidemic
guilty erethism
guilty excess
guilty immorality
guilty impurity
guilty indolescence
guilty satisfaction
guilty sensual pleasure
guilty touching
habit
habitual abuse
habitual auto-eroticism
harmful habit
harmful manoeuvre
harmful play
harmful practice
harmfulness of the flesh
hateful habit
hateful manoeuvre
hateful practice
hereditary disease
hereditary ipsation
hereditary lewdness
hereditary practice
hereditary scourge
hereditary vice
heterosexual substitute
hideous enormity
hideous habit
hideous mania
hideous substitute
homicidal hand
horrible habit
horrible manoeuvre
horrible phenomenon
horror
hostile offence
human misery
human weakness
humiliation of nature
hygenic habit
hypocritical horror
hysterical outrage
hysterical paroxysm
illegitimate excretion
illicit excretion
illicit hygiene
illicit jouissance
illicit manoeuvre

illicit pleasure
illness of ringed eyes
imaginative nervous diathesis
immature act
immature sexuality
immaturity
immoral act
immoral offence
impure sensation
impure touching
impurity
impurity with oneself
incestuous fantasy
incomplete expression
incomplete genitality
incomplete sexuality
inconceivable dissoluteness
independent love
independent pleasure
indignant debauchery
indignity
indiscreet trade
individual pleasure
infamous custom
infamous debauchery
infamous frenzy
infamous habit
infamous passion
infamous practice
infamy
infanticide
infantilism
inferior jouissance
inferior pleasure
infernal epidemic
infernal horror
inhibition
iniquitous murder
injurious habit
innocent pleasure
insane habit
insatiable appetite
instinctual manifestation
instinctual tendency
interior lust
intimate distress
intractable deviance
ipsation
ipsationism
ipsiation
irreligious gesture
irrepressible ardour
irrepressible pulsion
jerking-off
juvenile deviation
kind of debauchery
lascivious desire
lascivious idea
lascivious practice
last resort
legitimate substitute
leprosy

lethal act
lethal idleness
lewd act
lewd manifestation
lewd scandal
lewdness
liberating pleasure
libertinage manner
libidinal quasi-solipsism
licentious hand
limitless debauchery
loathsome act
loathsome depravity
loathsome subject
local excitement
love substitute
love with oneself
lust
lustful scene
luxuria
mad extravagance
malicious lust
maniac decadence
maniac jouissance
manic excess
manstupration
manual debauchery
manual excitation
manual excitement
manual pollution
manual prostitution
manual stain
manual touching
manual vice
manualization
manustupration
manusturbation
masculine obsession
masked deviation
mastupration
mastupration mania
masturbation
masturbomania
material act
maturative stage
means against nature
mechanical friction
mechanical sexuality
minute of vertigo
misery of humanity
mollities
moment of sin
momentary ipsation
monomaniac activity
monstrous selfishness
moral aberration
moral depravity
moral downfall
moral problem
morbid anxious practice
morbid auto-eroticism
morbid experience
morbid habit
morbid hyperactivity

morbid ingenuity
mortal illness
mortal lust
mortal sin
murder
narcissic habit
narcissic manoeuvre
narcissic neurosis
nasty manoeuvre
nasty ways
natural need
natural pulsion
natural soporific
necessary moment
necessary stage
nervous tic
neurosis of compensation
nocturnal enuresis
non-evasive misfortune
notorious perversion
obscene dance
obscene passion
obscene sensual pleasure
obsession
obvious vice
odious abuse
odious custom
odious habit
odious lust
odious manoeuvre
odious pleasure
Oedipean desire
offence against nature
offence to God
old habit
Onan infamy
onania
onanism
onanism vice
Onanistic manoeuvre
onanistic·practice
one man show
open wound
organic vice
original disease
original pleasure
outlet for fantasies
outrage to decency
outrage to nature
painful sensual pleasure
painful vacuity
para-natural act
para-natural pleasure
parapathy
paraphilia
paroxysmal pleasure
passion
passion against nature
peculiar danger
penile practice
pernicious crime
pernicious habit
pernicious practice
persistent vice

personal blossoming
personal equilibrium
perverse consummation
perverse dementia
perverse downfall
perverse manoeuvre
perverse play
perversion
perverted habit
petillomania
philosophical pleasure
physical downfall
physiological constraint
plague of society
pleasant alternative
pleasant itching
pleasure against nature
pleasure of the gods
pleasure of the schools
pleasuring oneself
pollution
pollution of the body
precocious deviance
pre-genital act
premature withering
primary experience
primitive behaviour
primitive need
private affair
prostitution
pseudo-coitus
pseudo-genital narcissism
pseudo-penetration
pseudo-plenitude
psychological lapse
public calamity
pure satisfaction
pure shameful act
rape of nature
raving recklessness
recklessness
refined debauchery
relief
renewed sin
renouncement of marriage
repeated touching
repetitive distraction
repetitive jerking
replacement activity
reputably large crime
revolting image
rhythmic movement
ridiculous pleasure
sacrilege
sad substitute
sap of cupidity
satanic pleasure
scholastic habit
school of abandon
scourge of the family
scourge of the world
secret act
secret conduct

secret crime
secret deviation
secret enormity
secret habit
secret lasciviousness
secret lewdness
secret prostitution
secret sin
secret touching
secret vice
self-abuse
self-disgust
selfish exercise
selfish pleasure
self-pollution
semen extra vas
semen mess
semi-morbid act
seminal loss
seminal squandering
senseless act
sensual stain
serious illness
serious moral disorder
serious offence
sexological trouble
sexual abuse
sexual autonomy
sexual exuberance
sexual habit
sexual hygiene
sexual illusion
sexual imperfection
sexual maturation
sexual misery
sexual need
sexual neurosis
sexual offence
sexual panacea
sexual psychopathy
sexual regression
shame
shame of oneself
shameful crime
shameful disease
shameful excess
shameful habit
shameful leaning
shameful leprosy
shameful manoeuvre
shameful misconduct
shameful overflowing
shameful passion
shameful pleasure
shameful practice
shameful relapse
shameful sensuality
shameful touching
shocking offence
sickly leaning
simple deviation
simple exonerating
gesture
sin against nature

sin against purity
sin of inertia
sin of laziness
sin of lust
sin of Onan
sin of slackness
sin of stain
sin of weakness
sin of youth
singular itching
slackness
small neurosis
smut
social crime
solitary action
solitary activity
solitary communion
solitary debauchery
solitary defect
solitary deviance
solitary deviation
solitary disease
solitary experience
solitary fiddling
solitary gymnastics
solitary habit
solitary hygiene
solitary jouissance
solitary leaning
solitary libertinage
solitary love
solitary madness
solitary manoeuvre
solitary orgasm
solitary passion
solitary play
solitary pleasure
solitary rapture
solitary research
solitary satisfaction
solitary sensual pleasure
solitary sensuality
solitary spasm
solitary vice
spermatic frenzy
squandering of energy
stain of oneself
stain of the flesh
stain of the night
sterile autism
sterile gesture
sterile mania
sterile pleasure
sterile sin
sterile substitute
stupid pleasure
subordinate activity
substitute
sui generis pleasure
suicidal act
suicide
superfluous practice
supreme disease
sustained fervour

sustained rubbing
sweet thing
systematic perversion
temptation of the flesh
the enormous
the habit
the only great habit
thumb-licking
to act against nature
true disease
type of pollution
tyrannical habit
tyranny of the habit
tyranny of the moment
unaccomplished desire
unalterable rite
unavowable impurity
unavowable manoeuvre
uncontrollable constraint
uncontrollable passion
unfinished sexuality
unforgiveable vice
unfortunate leaning
unfortunate manoeuvre
unfortunate unawareness
unhappy act
unhappy state
unhealthy mental projection
unhealthy turgescence
universal sin
unknown pleasure
unmistakable perversion
unmistakable sexual neurosis
unrepentant weakness
unrestrained gesture
usual madness
usual slavery
venereal abuse
venereal excess
venereal offence
very simple thing
vice
vice against nature
vice of pre-puberty
vice of schools
vice of the first years
vigorous massage
vile spectacle
vile substitute
voluntary eruption
voluntary pollution
voluntary precipice
voluntary spermatorrhoea
voluptuous caress
voluptuous spasm
voluptuous touching
waiting conduct
wanking
withdrawal
withdrawing
wretched misdeamenour